GLADIATORIA

MEDIEVAL ARMOURED COMBAT

DIERK HAGEDORN · BARTŁOMIEJ WALCZAK

GLADIATORIA
MEDIEVAL ARMOURED COMBAT

The 1450 Fencing Manuscript from New Haven

FOREWORD BY SYDNEY ANGLO

This edition published in 2018 by Greenhill Books,
c/o Pen & Sword Books Ltd,
47 Church Street, Barnsley, S. Yorkshire, S70 2AS
www.greenhillbooks.com

First published in 2015 by VS-BOOKS Torsten Verhülsdonk
Postfach 200540, 44635 Herne, Germany
www.vs-books.de

ISBN 978-1-78438-333-6

Library of Congress Cataloging-in-Publication data available

Typeset in Arno and Myriad by Dierk Hagedorn

Images used by kind permission of the
Yale Center for British Art, Paul Mellon Collection.

Printed and bound in India by Replika Press Pvt. Ltd.

for
Helen, Henri & Liliana

Dierk Hagedorn, born in 1966, is a designer of user interfaces, corporate design, and printed works. He is an instructor for the longsword at Hammaborg, a club that concentrates on reconstructing the historical European martial arts. He has transcribed more than twenty German fencing-related manuscripts and has made them publicly available on the Hammaborg website. He has published extensive volumes about some of the most important German manuscripts, such as the *Peter von Danzig* fightbook, the *Lew the Jew* fightbook, and the famous illustrated codex by Hans Talhoffer. In partnership with Bartłomiej Walczak, he has edited another *Gladiatoria* manuscript: a facsimile of the Cracow version. Other publications include numerous articles in magazines and essays for catalogues and anthologies. He is a member of the *Historical European Martial Arts Coalition* and has given many workshops and lectures about historical fencing with a particular focus on combat in armour in various countries.

Bartłomiej Walczak, born 1978, is a freelance film editor, visual effects artist, and colourist. Historical European Martial Arts have been his passion since 1999, and his work with the technical sources began in 2000. He founded and headed the Polish chapter of ARMA; co-founded the Polish HEMA Federation FEDER; he has taught and lectured worldwide and participated in tournaments, including winning the ILHG Open Longsword competition in 2015. He is also one of the founding members of the *HEMAC (Historical European Martial Arts Coalition)*. In 2002, he and Grzegorz Żabiński published *Codex Wallerstein: A Medieval Fighting Book from the Fifteenth Century*. Other publications include a preface to the facsimile edition of the *Gladiatoria* version from Cracow (with Dierk Hagedorn) and the Polish translation of *Peter von Danzig* (with Grzegorz Żabiński and Monika Maziarz). His areas of expertise include unarmoured and armoured longsword and dagger.

CONTENTS

ACKNOWLEDGEMENTS

The book that you are about to enjoy is the result of our seemingly endless efforts to do justice to what we believe to be one of the very finest surviving medieval illustrated manuscripts.

Years ago—quite some time before we got to know each other—we independently stumbled over an astounding manuscript with truly stunning artwork: The *Gladiatoria* manuscript from Cracow, which is very similar to the one we present to you here. We were mesmerised by the combination of astonishing illustrations and profound explanations of the described techniques, all performed in full armour. Subsequently, a second *Gladiatoria* exemplar from Vienna came to our attention, as did other related manuscripts with *Gladiatoria* material that were also similar, yet with the difference that they contained little or no text. For quite some time we worked independently on the manuscripts of the *Gladiatoria* group, until finally, more than a decade ago, we met at an international fencing event, discovered our mutual love and admiration for the *Gladiatoria* group, and instantly decided to join forces. By that time, the *Gladiatoria* manuscript from a library in Gotha, Germany, which was believed to be lost during World War II, had resurfaced in the United States and was ready for a close examination.

With our combined efforts, we endeavoured to tackle the intricacies, the similarities and the differences of all of the *Gladiatoria* codices—a task that ultimately proved too demanding. Finally, we decided to concentrate solely on the New Haven manuscript, having chosen it as the most worthy for our edition.

It took us more than five years, during which this book has changed many times, sometimes drastically. In 2015, however, the synergy of our efforts and our mutual support throughout this long process allowed us to finally present the fruits of our labour in a bilingual German–English edition: the reproduction of the earliest representative of the *Gladiatoria* line. While neither as mature as the Cracow version, nor as complete as the Vienna one, it contains the widest variety of early 15th century arms and armour, depicted in amazing detail. At the same time, the codex has an intriguing history of its own. We hope to have done it justice—both visually and academically.

But the story doesn't end there. Two years later, we were approached by Michael Leventhal of Greenhill Books: could we imagine a revised edition that would keep the English text—and the beautiful artwork, of course—but drop the German text? Of course, we agreed. The splendour of *Gladiatoria* should be spread, and the knowledge about it should grow and prosper.

We would not have been able to succeed without the invaluable help of friends and colleagues worldwide. Therefore, particular thanks go to Martin Austwick, Jörg Bellinghausen, Michael Chidester, Tomasz Ciaciek, Keith Farrell, Matthias Goll, Cornelia Hopf, Daniel Jaquet, Jens Peter Kleinau, Krzysztof Kruczyński, Francis Lapka, Gregory Mele, Ireneusz Nowak, David Rawlings, Radosław Ropka, Julia Thut, Manuel Valle Ortiz, Roland Warzecha, Martin Wierschin, Thore Wilkens, Hagen Wooge, and Grzegorz Żabiński.

We want to emphasise the tremendous assistance of Christian H. Tobler, who generously helped with proof-reading the English versions of all texts for the first edition.

We also need to point out the remarkable amendments and pieces of advice we owe to Elani K. Wales, who checked every sentence in concert with the German text and suggested numerous enhancements.

Another huge thank you goes to our publishers, Torsten Verhülsdonk of the original edition, without whom the whole affair would have ended as an unfulfillable dream, and Michael Leventhal, who insisted on a revised version.

And finally, very special thanks go to our beloved and patient wives, Verena and Urszula.

We are happy and grateful that our field of expertise and our ongoing efforts towards making the old manuscripts shine seem to gather an audience. We owe you much, dear reader.

Dierk Hagedorn and Bartłomiej Walczak

February 2018

SYDNEY ANGLO

FOREWORD

SYDNEY ANGLO

FOREWORD

Early in the 16th century the once-forgotten but now famous Spanish master of arms Pietro Monte declared that skills such as wrestling and the effective handling of weapons in personal combat could not be acquired solely through words. Practical demonstration by an expert was an absolute necessity. And, apart from a few eccentric exceptions, other masters of arms similarly felt that, without the help of a teacher, their skills could not be adequately acquired by students—however keen and able the latter might be. Yet many of these martial pedagogues were moved to set forth their fighting arts in treatises comprehensive in scope and frequently illustrated by artwork of considerable sophistication and exactitude; and the *Gladiatoria* manuscript—impeccably edited in this present volume—is an especially noteworthy example of the genre.

Neither Monte nor any other master established a school or tradition enduring enough to provide for modern students the practical demonstrations once thought indispensable, and nowadays the enthusiast is obliged to deduce whatever is possible from the manuscripts and early printed books which survive in libraries and other repositories and which are still available for study. For several years now the importance of these fightbooks prepared by masters of arms throughout the late Middle Ages and Renaissance has been recognized by scholars anxious to reconstruct the martial arts of Western Europe—although, unfortunately, outside that circle of enthusiasts, the value of these texts has not been widely recognised. That is why I am delighted to have been invited to contribute a foreword to this edition which offers precisely the approach and information that is badly needed not only to enlighten students of historic martial arts but also to attract the attention of other scholars who have thus far resolutely ignored the sort of material which is so elegantly laid out before us by the editors of this volume.

In the first place, their analysis of the manuscript's structure makes clear, and resolves, the considerable difficulties to be encountered in any attempt at establishing the original state of such an elaborate codex and its relationship to other texts. But this edition is exemplary in other ways too. While it is true that there has recently been a spate of published versions of fight manuscripts and early fencing texts, many of these have been designed for a limited readership which is not particularly concerned with scholarship or with intellectual considerations beyond the actual reconstruction of fighting techniques. Thus there have been several translations displaying varying degrees of accuracy; with silent emendations; with sketchy and elementary introductions stating little beyond the obvious; and even with adulterated illustrations. An edition such as the present volume is much rarer—although fortunately becoming less so.[1] It not only provides a high-quality facsimile reproduction of the original pictures and text; but it also offers a transcript of that text; an annotated translation into modern German and English; and an analytical study of the codex itself, clarifying matters of provenance, structure, binding and trimming, and similar essential technical information. All of this enables readers to grasp the way in which the original work evolved and, of course, to use their own intelligence and experience to tease out the most likely practical interpretation of obscure or ambiguous passages.

However, a publication such as this raises other important issues which should not be overlooked. It is evident that the written exposition of the combatants' movements and postures are here as exact as mere words can make them; and the illustrations which accompany each verbal description are meticulous and expertly drawn. Indeed the artwork clarifies not only the sequence of movements in a general way but also pays close attention to every gesture; to leg and foot placement; to the movement and position of hands and even of the fingers; and, of course, to the constantly changing relationships between spears, swords, and daggers. Moreover, each section of this text—as in most other combat manuals—constantly refers the reader to the relevant illustration for clarification. 'As you see painted above' is the refrain on all but three folios. The marriage of word and image is paramount: but I wonder (not for the first time) whether any notice will be taken of this and similar books either by art historians or by historians of pedagogy. Cohorts of the former would certainly cluster around a manuscript of similar date and quality were it devoted to the lives of saints

1 Among the more valuable editions I would note FORGENG: *The Medieval Art of Swordsmanship*; RUBBOLI/CESARI: *Flos Duellatorum*; ŻABIŃSKI/WALCZAK: *Codex Wallerstein*; and PORZIO/MELE: *Arte Gladiatoria Dimicandi.*

rather than to the activities of knights engaged in personal combat. Similarly scholars, who have often noted the stress placed by Renaissance educationalists on the need for physical and military training, never seem to have noticed that what we have in works such as *Gladiatoria* is an advanced, sophisticated pedagogical system of movement notation expounding those very skills which were deemed crucial throughout the Renaissance and beyond. It is to be hoped that art historians and students of so-called 'Humanism' will recognize the inherent value of such records and not shrink from the violence of personal combat especially when it is as intelligently and beautifully presented as in the manuscript here under consideration. Certainly students of Western martial arts—many of whom *are* aesthetically aware and historically informed—will give it the attention it deserves.

DIERK HAGEDORN

OFFENCE & DEFENCE

DIERK HAGEDORN

OFFENCE AND DEFENCE

Arms and Armour from the New Haven *Gladiatoria* Manuscript

We all know what a knight looks like: a shiny suit of armour covers his body, and in his hand he holds a mighty sword, exactly like a Playmobil figure or another toy knight, exactly as we may have seen in the movies. The fighters in the *Gladiatoria* manuscript from New Haven wear magnificent armour too, and they are equipped with all kinds of weapons. In this brief outline I want to concentrate primarily on the peculiarities and the characteristics of arms and armour of this particular manuscript; a thorough and detailed examination remains to be done—essentially due to mere reasons of space.

I. ARMOUR

The Harness

Armour, or, to use the more historically accurate term, the harness[1] (plate 1) that dresses an entire man[2] in iron plates, appeared only at the very end of the age of chivalry. When the development of the complete suit of plate armour was completed, the

1 The term "harness", from Old French "harnois", generally refers to the body protection, which develops from mail into plate armour. Another specific term is the cuirass, which consists only of breast- and backplate.

2 Evidence of women in armour is extremely rare. The painter called "Meister des Albrechtsaltars zu Klosterneuburg" for example depicts the Virgin Mary in harness. However, this is obviously intended as an allegory. A well-known portrait of a prominent harness wearer, Joan of Arc, was created by an unknown artist, although not in her lifetime (Paris, Centre Historique des Archives Nationales).

decline of knighthood had already begun and other power factors, such as trade and commerce in the cities, were becoming increasingly important. Nevertheless, harnesses continued to be used for centuries before ultimately being phased out. Very occasionally, however, harness wearers appear even today—such as the Swiss Guards of the Pope, who are still equipped with a breastplate.

The development from body protection made of mail to a complete plate harness[3] took place mainly in what is now northern Italy, largely in the second half of the 14th century.[4] After that time, no substantial new features were added; however, wearing comfort was improved and the protective effect increased by more refined and sophisticated technical details.[5] The shoulder constituted a particular challenge in this respect.[6] Further changes were often only fashionable whims,[7] such as exuberant fluting, etching, gilding and other accumulations of decoration in what was referred to as parade armor. Around 1420, the development of the Italian harness was largely completed. At the time, the "soft style" predominated in Germany; this term describes the appearance of armour that consists of a combination of individual iron plates, fabric, and parts made of mail.[8]

Unfortunately, very few specimens have survived from the period spanning the early days of the armourer's art to about the middle of the 15th century,[9] and an exact number is next to impossible to ascertain.[10] Early harnesses made in Italy appear relatively frequently. This is due to the division of labour in the production process, which allowed for enormous output. The German armourers, who were organized in

3 The rigidity of overlapping steel plates gives greater protection than the by-then penetrable surface of mail, particularly against strikes. Individual parts made of metal plates, such as poleyns and greaves, already existed in the 13th century (FLIEGEL: *Arms & Armor*, p. 44).

4 The smiths who produced armour, the armourers, established themselves in all major cities. By the demands placed on them in a technical and artistic point of view, they distinguished themselves from the mass of metal-working craftsmen and artisans (*Die Innsbrucker Plattnerkunst*, p. 17).

5 GOLL, MÜLLER, GRAF: "Die älteste deutsche Harnischbrust. Ein Sensationsfund?" p. 36.

6 KÜHNEL (EDITOR): *Bildwörterbuch der Kleidung und Rüstung*, p. lxxvii.

7 BOEHEIM: *Handbuch der Waffenkunde*, p. 145.

8 KÜHNEL (EDITOR): *Bildwörterbuch der Kleidung und Rüstung*, p. lxxviii.

9 Approximately 95 per cent of the preserved armour comes from the period after the battle of Agincourt in 1415 (FLIEGEL: *Arms & Armor*, p. 21).

10 GOLL: *Mit eiserner Faust*, p.14.

strictly regulated guilds, could not accomplish this to that extent. Notable examples can be found in the armoury of Churburg castle in Schluderns (South Tirol)[11] which possesses the oldest surviving breastplate from about 1370 (inv. no. CHS 13). This breastplate came from the workshop of the famous armourer family Missaglia (plate 2). At this time harnesses made in Italy were far superior to examples from Germany.[12]

By around the middle of the 15th century, the competing armouring centres in Italy and Germany had developed their particular own style. Italian harnesses are smooth and rounded. By contrast, the German harnesses are far more angular and edgy. The surface of the individual armour parts were increasingly decorated with ridges and flutings.[13] Around the year 1470, this eventually led to the so-called "Gothic" armour style, a term, however, that stems from the Victorian age. With its intricacy and graceful exterior appearance, it "represents the apogée of the armourer's art".[14]

The Italian harness also differs from German examples in some construction-related peculiarities: it has lateral fastenings consisting of hinges (left) and buckles (right), and articulated breast and backplates connected by leather straps. The shoulder defences, called pauldrons, are expansive and asymmetrical, and the most popular helmet is the visored armet.

German armour parts from the mid-15th century are much rarer than Italian ones, and not even a single complete suit has survived. The best preserved one is a composite of two harnesses from about 1450 in the Wien Museum in Vienna (inv. no. 127.000–127.009), but the pauldrons, rerebraces, couters, gauntlets and helmet are missing (plate 3).[15] It ranks among the so-called "Kastenbrust" harnesses that feature

---

11 Detailed photos in Boccia: *Le armature … del '400.*

12 Lehnart: *Kleidung & Waffen der Spätgotik III, 1420–1480*, p. 92.

13 Capwell: *The Real Fighting Stuff*, p. 21.

14 Edge/Paddock: *Arms & Armor of the Medieval Knight*, p. 103.

15 "On closer inspection, the unfortunately incomplete equestrian armour turns out to consist of the remnants of two contemporaneous harnesses. One of them, the slightly larger one, was manufactured with a plain surface, only enlivened by jagged edges on the movable bands—the so-called "lames", the other one was decorated by radiating ridges and flutings, and by notched edges on the lames. The bulging chest with three vertical ridges and a culet that reached down to the groin, initially belonged to the plain armour. Today it lacks the riveted strips on the rims of the arm defences and the cottered lancerest on the right side of the breastplate. In addition, the greaves, including the sabatons, belong to this armour; and finally the vambraces, being the remainders of a formerly movably assembled arm defence,

a more or less box-shaped breastplate and which were popular in the Holy Roman Empire and in Flanders. The origin of the term Kastenbrust (or "box-shaped breast") remains unknown, but it alludes to the geometrical ideal (a straight, flat chest, that bends inwards almost in a right angle just below the breastbone), although deviations seem to be the rule rather than the exception.

The expression Kastenbrust is thus somewhat misleading because the surviving specimens are not particularly box-shaped, but have rather bulbous or bulged forms, sometimes even with a pronounced middle ridge. Thus, the only four surviving examples correspond only partially to the definition as it is provided, for instance, in the *Bildwörterbuch der Kleidung und Rüstung*: the Kastenbrust is a prismatic shaped breastplate with transverse and lateral edges as a part of the late Gothic harness from the mid-15th century, also comprising a tonlet.[16] Another characteristic of the Kastenbrust is the one-piece construction of the breastplate, which, unlike the later articulated examples, overlaps a waist plate from above at roughly navel height. In contrast, the articulated lames of later harnesses are constructed such that each lower plate overlaps the upper one. The surviving examples suggest that the tonlet that is attached to the lower edge can be taken off by means of pins and clips if required.

Another Kastenbrust from the Metropolitan Museum in New York (inv. no. 29.150.79) is also not particularly box-shaped. The surface is broken up by numerous small ridges that extend radially from the bottom edge of the breastplate up to the armholes. Another specimen, in the Glasgow Museums (inv. no. A1981.40.a–c), is dated to 1430–50 and is considered to be the earliest surviving piece.[17] While it is clearly much more box-shaped, it nevertheless shows strongly rounded shapes at the sides of the abdomen.

A few years ago, Matthias Goll succeeded in identifying another Kastenbrust at the Deutsches Historisches Museum in Berlin (inv. no. W2312).[18] Due to the diversity

were added to this composite late Gothic suit of armour. The other harness provided the backplate including a short culet, decorated with embossed ridges—again missing the riveted strips—as well as the upper leg defences (cuisses), and finally the greaves including sabatons from the late Gothic armour." (*Das Wiener Bürgerliche Zeughaus*, p. 39.)

16 KÜHNEL (ED.): *Bildwörterbuch der Kleidung und Rüstung*, p. 131.

17 CAPWELL: *The Real Fighting Stuff*, p. 21.

18 GOLL/MÜLLER/GRAF: "Die älteste deutsche Harnischbrust. Ein Sensationsfund?"

of those harnesses summarized under the term Kastenbrust, Goll, Müller and Graf suggest a variety of more refining terms: "straight Kastenbrust" for the classic square type, "articulated Kastenbrust" for variants with multiple lames instead of a single waist plate, and "Kastenbrust with a middle ridge".

Sources from the visual arts are far more numerous than actual surviving examples: paintings by artists such as Rogier van der Weyden (plate 4), Jan van Eyck, Hans Multscher, Master Francke, and Konrad Witz show early harnesses in loving detail, even and especially those with a Kastenbrust. Some sculptures depict elaborate Kastenbrust armour in detail, such as the statue of St. George from the main altar of St. George Church in Wismar (plate 5).

The manuscripts of the *Gladiatoria* group[19] stem from the transitional period around the middle of the 15th century, when the soft style merged into the Gothic style.[20] Precise dating of the manuscripts is difficult, but if one takes the stylistic criteria of armour into consideration—the remarkable similarity with the painting "Virgin and Child with Canon van der Paele" by Jan van Eyck from 1436 is particularly striking—dating to exactly this period is rather likely. The three *Gladiatoria* manuscripts containing both images and text (Cracow, New Haven, and Vienna), are generally quite similar to each other—although the Cracow codex does stand out, both in terms of the illustrations as well as the stern *textualis* handwriting, making its appearance more sophisticated but also more stylised. The two specimens from Vienna and New Haven are much more similar to each other, and it even seems that the scribe responsible for the New Haven codex wrote large parts of the Vienna version.[21] The quality of the illustrations in the New Haven manuscript is consistently higher than in the

19 Named for the Cracow manuscript *Ms. Berol. germ. quart. 16* which carries the term "Gladiatoria" (= sword fighting) on the title page in capital letters.

20 Hans-Peter Hils dated the New Haven codex (then still believed to be lost in the war) loosely to the 15th century in general, the manuscript from Cracow to the first half of the 15th century, and the one from Vienna to about the year 1430. The Wolfenbüttel codex is also dated to the 15th century, and the former Donaueschingen manuscript, which is currently located in Paris, is labelled as a compilation written around the year 1500 (Hils: *Meister Johann Liechtenauers Kunst des langen Schwertes*).

21 Two writers were involved in the creation of the Vienna manuscript *KK 5013* (Frühmorgen-Voss/Ott/Bodemann/Stöllinger-Löser/Leng: *Katalog der deutschsprachigen illustrierten Handschriften des Mittelalters.* Band 4/2, Lieferung 1/2, p. 30).

one from Vienna, although there are nevertheless some outstanding exceptions (folios 7r/v, 11r/v, 17v–19r, 28r/v, 31v and 49r/v).

The variety of the harnesses in the two manuscripts from New Haven and Vienna is significantly larger than in the Cracow version, where the armour appears rather schematic and uniformly drawn. In particular, the New Haven codex offers the greatest wealth of armour details. The fighters in this manuscript still wear some textile armour parts or larger amounts of mail pieces—almost every harness wearer has a mail skirt. Even on harnesses of a much later origin, some parts of the body are still protected with mail made of small metal rings, such as where it is difficult or impossible for the plates to cover spots such as the armpits, the crooks of the arm, or the crotch. This flexible mesh was naturally more susceptible to strikes, but the sword's tip would stop in the tiny gaps of the small rings. And thus Martin Huntfelt, for instance, expressly recommends in his instructions for the "Kampffechten"[22] (harness fencing, literally: combat fencing), which are preserved in several fencing treatises, that combatants put the sword into the opponent's rings (for example, Rome, Biblioteca dell'Accademia Nazionale dei Lincei e Corsiniana, *44 A 8*, folio 89r).

The greatest opulence of variations is seen in the armour of the upper body. Here, the construction method cannot always be clearly seen in the illustrations, especially where a textile surcoat veils the breastplate. However, there are breast and backplates that seem to be riveted together from numerous vertical segments (for example, folios 10v, 11r, 15v, and 16r), some that are reminiscent of a brigandine (folios 16v, 23v, and 25r), and fully formed plate defences as well (folios 11r, 24v, 38r, 40v, 43r). Only a few examples depict a torso defence made of mail (folios 7r, 23r, 34v, 35r), and combinations (such as mail armour with a single breastplate, folio 36v) also appear sporadically. A curiosity is present in the left fighter on folio 28r, whose abdomen is protected beneath the breastplate with a mail skirt, which then, however, continues below the opponent's arm in front as a fauld of articulated lames—probably due to inattention on the part of the illustrator. Incidentally, we shall meet this gentleman again elsewhere.

The majority of breastplates shown are curved and round, but there are quite a number of examples of armour which correspond to the Kastenbrust type—sometimes more pronounced, sometimes less—for example, here in the New Haven man-

22 In the fencing treatises, the usual expression for the duel in armour.

uscript on folios 3v, 8v, 11r, 24v, and 25r; and in the Vienna manuscript on folios 4v, 18v, and 19r.

The leg defences are nearly uniform, with the exception of the sabatons, some of which are scaled, partially made of mail, or partially constructed of articulated lames. On several leg defences there is also a detail that is usually only found in Italian Quattrocento[23] harnesses: a perforated metal band, riveted to the lower lame of the poleyn, to which a slim strip of mail is attached.

The arm defences are also very similar to each other. The shoulder represents a transitional form from the smaller spaudlers that just cover the shoulders, to the much wider pauldrons, equipped with sweeping front and rear wings.

Considering the period of origin of the codex, the low-worn plaque belts are also noteworthy, as they already look a bit old-fashioned, although they still seem to have been used to some degree (see plate 5). The sheaths for dagger and sword are attached to these.

Other aspects of particular interest are the buckles on the back of each of the right fencers on folios 1v and 24r, which may represent a helmet attachment; a unique lance rest on the left fighter on folio 28r—the gentleman with the two-part groin protection (in the entire *Gladiatoria* group there is no second lance rest to be found); a heavy chain on folio 34r on the right armoured fencer, reaching from the right shoulder across the abdomen to the left calf;[24] not clearly identifiable fasteners on the right side of the harness of the left fighter on folio 38r; and finally a plaque belt, cluttered with small bells, at the left fencer on folio 5v.

The *Gladiatoria* harnesses represent armour for combat on foot for which symmetrical pauldrons are typical. The pauldrons of equestrian harnesses are often cut out on the right side in order to accommodate the insertion of the lance into the lance rest.

23 The time of the early Renaissance in Italy, the 15th century.

24 The meaning of this chain is not apparent. Earlier armour has chains attached not only to the breastplate, but also to both sword and dagger in order to prevent them from getting lost during fighting. One particular chain can be admired that is located on or around the neck of a field harness from the Dresden Armoury. This is, however, "a souvenir of the encirclement of Duke Heinrich by the Frisians in Franeker in the year 1500, which was originally kept separately and does not belong to the harness, which can only have been manufactured in the second decade of the 16th century at the earliest." (*Harnische. Historisches Museum Dresden*, p. 51.)

On the left shoulder, which was more exposed to attacks, however, the pauldron frequently reaches down lower.[25] Another characteristic feature is the tonlet that is formed from the abdominal lames of the fauld, and the culet which occasionally can even reach down to the knee.[26] Although the lance rest mentioned on folio 28r indicates an equestrian harness, it is not impossible that the same armour could be worn for combat both on horseback and on foot. It is possible that even early harnesses were already specially assembled for the intended use, something that becomes rather common somewhat later, from the 16th century onwards, with the extensive armour sets, so-called garnitures, which may consist of more than 100 individual pieces. Another indication for the use on foot are cuisses that are closed at the rear (for example, folio 42v), which do not exist for fights on horseback, as this would make it difficult or even impossible to steer a horse due to the lack of contact of the thigh with the body of the horse.

Construction and Wearing Comfort[27]

Several specialized craftsmen were involved in the production of a harness. In addition to the armourer, responsible for the forging of the steel plates and generally bringing the metal into shape, there was the polisher and others who attended to the leather strapping and the gloves. The edges of the individual armour parts were reinforced in numerous places by bending them over a wire; also, not all parts of a plate were the same thickness. Often those portions facing the opponent, such as the front of the breastplate, were thicker than the lateral parts. After forging, the harness was mounted on a trial basis in order to achieve the best possible fit. Finally, the individual parts were joined with loosely connected sliding rivets[28] and leather straps, resulting in a flexible and yet stable body armour.[29] Stephen N. Fliegel writes: "The armor

25 KÜHNEL (EDITOR): *Bildwörterbuch der Kleidung und Rüstung*, p. 81.

26 KÜHNEL (EDITOR): *Bildwörterbuch der Kleidung und Rüstung*, p. 268.

27 Ulrich Lehnart provides a very detailed description of the armour styles and parts of the aforementioned time frame in *Kleidung & Waffen der Spätgotik III, 1420–1480*.

28 Oblong slots in two overlapping metal plates allow the sliding rivets to move back and forth, so that the plates can shift further from each other than would be possible with simple circular holes.

29 *Meisterwerke der Hofjagd- und Rüstkammer*, p. 33f.

plates were ingeniously pivoted to each other at the sides by sliding rivets that moved in slots. The elements of a suit of armor were never riveted directly to each other (since this would render them inflexible), but were made to overlap slightly. Within the concealed areas were the rivets securing them to interior leather straps. The exterior rivets were either sliding rivets or nonfunctional ornamental rivets."[30]

There were indeed harnesses "off the shelf", bought and sold by distributors and merchants. A better fit, however, was of course guaranteed by custom-made armour, which was facilitated by the customer's personal garments being provided to the armourer.[31] Bruno Thomas writes: "The harness is accurately made to measure—either from measurements of the customer himself or of his clothes, which are sent to the armorer—for one single wearer and his unique dimensions. Only he completely fills his form. Only with him can the armour fulfill its full purpose."[32]

The armourer transformed rigid metal parts into a flexible structure, almost a sculpture, that only showed its true beauty once its owner put it on and brought it to life. According to Bruno Thomas once again: "You can pick a single piece, such as a gauntlet, individually and study the rich, shaped play of movement in its many steel bands. The armourer pursues every single joint and its mode of action. Indeed, he manages to surpass it significantly in most cases. The body was to be given the opportunity to perform its gestures, and to find its shaped expression within its own movements—unhindered by a steel garment. Moreover, the harnesses made by the great masters strive to support this expression, and even to increase it. In truth, they are able to raise their wearers beyond themselves, to monumentalise them."[33]

The Weight of Armour

Mobility in armour and the weight of armour are constant sources of popular misconception. In a life or death battle, hardly anyone would take the chance of sacrificing the essential ability to move freely strictly in favour of protection. In fact, mobil-

30 Fliegel: *Arms & Armor,* p. 45f.
31 Norman: *Waffen und Rüstungen,* p. 41f.
32 Thomas: *Deutsche Plattnerkunst,* p. 18.
33 Thomas: *Deutsche Plattnerkunst,* p. 17.

ity in armour was fundamental and was only slightly impaired. Recent studies at the University of Geneva have shown that some movement patterns allow even greater freedom with armour than without it.[34]

Likewise, the weight of armour is usually estimated far too high. If we take the field pack of a modern soldier, which can weigh 30 kg or more, depending on the country and the mission, the burden rests primarily on the shoulders. However, the weight of the medieval harness was distributed over the entire body in a beneficial way. Indeed, this makes the use of the arms and legs slightly cumbersome, but overall, it offered considerable wearing comfort—especially for someone used to wearing armour from their youth.

Since, unfortunately, complete originals from the mid-15th century have not survived, we can only use whole harnesses from later periods for comparison. The armour for field and tournament from 1505–10 (W 81.12,30.94) from the Deutsches Historisches Museum in Berlin, for instance, weighs only 19.9 kg[35] and would still remain below 30 kg, even with the addition of clothing worn underneath, mail armour parts, sword and dagger. Another suit of armour from about 1520 from the same museum (W 2326, 38.226) weighs 22.4 kg[36] and a third from about 1540 (W 2325 a–h, 06.658 a–m) weighs only 18.9 kg[37]—but this one is missing the left gauntlet. One heavyweight of the museum is the "Riefelharnisch"—as harnesses with an abundance of mostly vertical and parallel flutings are called—W 2327, AD 2997, which weighs in at 26.8 kg on the scales, but then again it is also 188 cm tall.[38] The closest chronological relative is a Gothic field harness from about 1470 (W 1052, AB 1397), which, however, is equipped with arm defenses that are not originally from this field harness, but rather from jousting armour, and the weight of which totals 22.7 kg.[39]

The immobile knight, who, as soon as he has gone to ground, cannot rise again, and who would need to be lifted onto his horse by crane in any case, is an unfortunate legend that we owe to Laurence Olivier's motion picture *Henry V*, which is otherwise quite worth watching.

34 JAQUET: *Combattre en armure à la fin du Moyen Âge et au début de la Renaissance d'après l'étude des livres de combat.*

35 QUAAS: *Eisenkleider*, p. 65.

36 QUAAS: *Eisenkleider*, p. 65.

37 QUAAS: *Eisenkleider*, p. 83.

38 QUAAS: *Eisenkleider*, p. 85.

39 QUAAS: *Eisenkleider*, p. 46.

In fact, while there was indeed heavy armour, it was generally only used for tournaments. In particular, helmets could reach an enormous weight of 15 kg—in contrast to the "normal" helmet, which weighed only 2–3 kg. However, the tournament was a highly specialised sport that required highly specialised equipment that could not be considered as a benchmark for field harnesses.[40]

Safety

The harness provided its wearer with excellent all-around protection. However, absolute safety could not be ensured even here, because some parts of the body simply cannot be covered with steel plates. Examples include the leather gloves inside the gauntlets, which are necessary to grip the weapon securely, and the soles of shoes, because of the need for traction. In particular, the vision slits and vents in the visor were indispensable. These vulnerabilities, called openings, were naturally preferred targets for attack in combat. The fencing master Johannes Liechtenauer, for instance, lists the following openings: "Merck das ist wo der gewappent man am pesten zw gewinenn ist durch den harnasch | das ist vnder dem gesicht oder vnder den v̈chsen | Oder In den tanär der hendt oder auf dem arm̃ hinden Inn den hantschuechen oder in den knÿkelen oder vnden an den fuessen den süllen | vnd In den gelencken der armpüg | vnd zwischen den painen | vnd an den steten da der harnasch sein gelenck hat | vnd die plössen soltu also suechen das dw zw einer ferreren nicht solt arbaitten noch stechen | wenn dw ein nahere vor dir gehaben magst".[41] (Note, this tells where the best places are to attack an armoured man through the harness. These are under the face, under the armpits, in the palms of the hands, on the arms from behind into the gauntlets, into the hollows of the knee, or below on the soles of the feet, in the insides of the elbows, between the legs, and anywhere the harness has its articulations. And you should seek the openings such that you do not work or thrust to a more distant opening when you can reach a closer one.)[42]

Apart from that, the harness did protect the wearer very effectively against wounding, and a stroke or a thrust to the smooth and rounded plates was virtually ineffective and would not penetrate the steel. Nevertheless, there are several histori-

40 Lehnart: *Kleidung & Waffen der Spätgotik III, 1420–1480*, p. 78.

41 Rome, Biblioteca dell'Accademia Nazionale dei Lincei e Corsiniana, *44 A 8*, folio 58v.

42 Tobler: *In Saint George's Name*, Wheaton, 2010.

cal depictions of destroyed, pierced, battered, or smashed harnesses.[43] The question of how realistic penetrations such as these are is much discussed, especially since surviving specimens are rather rare.[44] To use modern replicas for verification may not necessarily provide a clear conclusion, because of different materials and manufacturing processes; sacrificing valuable originals is obviously not an option. So we look with great interest upon the punctured armours in the Wolfenbüttel *Gladiatoria* manuscript in which we can see breastplates being pierced with daggers on folios 82r , 94v (plate 8), 105v, 107v, and 110r; and on folio 109v, a helmet is completely pierced (plate 9). Other *Gladiatoria* versions do not show destroyed armour parts.

The Helmet

Since all four extant Kastenbrust harnesses have survived only rudimentarily, we cannot say with certainty what type of helmet originally belonged to them. Paintings and sculptures suggest, however, that they were associated either with a kettle hat or with a bascinet, often in a particular variant called the great bascinet. In a famous painting by Konrad Witz that depicts a complete Kastenbrust harness, the suit of armour is equipped with just such a great bascinet that incidentally bears several nicks and scratches on the helmet's skull.

The helmets of the *Gladiatoria* manuscripts all belong to a single, uniform type, and they are remarkably similar to each other throughout. All have the form of a visored helmet, which has certain similarities to the great bascinet, but also shows elements of a close-fitting armet or a German close helmet. However, due to the illustrated head position, a great bascinet seems unlikely, since it would be attached to the breast and backplate (often by leather straps), which indeed allows rotation of the head inside the helmet to a small extent, but never in concert with the helmet. On the other

43 In one of Talhoffer's manuscripts, for example, we can see breastplates being pierced with a pollaxe: Copenhagen, Det Kongelige Bibliotek, *Thott 290 20*, folios 132r and 134v (plate 6); and in the famous *Codex Manesse* (Heidelberg, Universitätsbibliothek, *Cod. Pal. germ. 848*, folio 321v) Dietmar der Setzer smashes the great helm of his opponent with a sword (plate 7).

44 The collection at Schloss Ambras in Innsbruck possesses a set of tournament armour, the helmet skull of which shows two pierced square holes on the left side.

hand, the straps on the back that appear in two illustrations have already been addressed, so a clear assertion is unfortunately impossible.

The visor is mainly depicted with two symmetrically arranged series of several narrow vertical vision slits; the circles that commonly appear above and beneath these slits can be interpreted either as decoration or as additional horizontal rows of air holes. The hinges of the visors are always covered with round discs.

Some helmets are shown with an aventail at the bottom, but this is not uniformly the case. While the manuscripts from New Haven and Vienna quite often show such aventails, they don't appear at all in the Cracow manuscript, with the exception of folio 30r. Other examples have either a throat and neck protection that apparently consists of articulated lames and that extends downwards to the breastplate (for example, folio 34r), or possibly a completely rigid protection.

The Gauntlets

It is noteworthy that some illustrated fencing manuscripts that deal with the armoured duel omit the presentation of steel gauntlets altogether. In the present manuscript, there are only two pictures in which the fighters wear gauntlets (folios 27r and 28v). These two pages normally follow each other directly and are only separated here due to the rebinding of the codex. It is only here that the gauntlet is explicitly mentioned as a target. It is not clear why no gauntlets are presented in the rest of the manuscript since the illustrator was quite capable of depicting hand positions, even with gauntlets. Illustrated gauntlets are also omitted in several manuscripts by Hans Talhoffer.[45] Other

45 The archetypal *Königsegg codex* (Königseggwald, Gräfliches Schloss, *Hs. XIX, 17–3*), for example, also dispenses with the presentation of gauntlets. With the exception of p. 7, where the hands have a natural colouring, they are provided with the same gray-blue washes as the armour. Special cases are the armed men praying on pages 3 and 45, which also have flesh-coloured hands without any gauntlets depicted in the image. On pages 18 and 43, however, we actually see gauntlets. In the former, Master Talhoffer helps squire Luithold of Königsegg to don his harness, with the squire holding a gauntlet at the cuff in his left hand, while his helmet is still on the ground. On page 48 the killed adversary is stripped of his armour, including gauntlets. Another representation of gauntlets is similar to that in the *Gladiatoria* group: The image for the text "das füren by dem hentschoch" shows a fighter leading his opponent out of the fight ring with the sword tip in the cuff. It is noteworthy that the armed men in the horse fighting section (pp. 99–119) also do not wear gauntlets and have naturally coloured hands.

manuscripts, both earlier and later ones, such as those by Jörg Wilhalm,[46] Ludwig von Eyb,[47] Paulus Kal,[48] the *Codex Wallerstein,*[49] the Berlin codex *Libr. pict. A 83,* but also the earliest Talhoffer manuscript from 1448[50]—to name just a few—indeed show armoured men with their gauntlets. The reason why the artists of the *Gladiatoria* manuscripts refrain from generally presenting gauntlets in the picture thus remains a mystery.

The cuffs of the few specimens, however, consistently have a plain hourglass form and, in contrast to those from the end of the 15th century, no articulation. Only the fingers are made of several small lames.

The Surcoats

A majority of the fighters wear long surcoats, which ornamentally frame the combat action in flowing shapes. Numerous dagged garments occur that embrace the harnesses tightly. It should be emphasized that the illustrated textiles snugly follow the shape of the breast and backplates, and that in some cases buttons (front: folios 4r, 5r, 6r, 9v, 11v, 12r, 13v, 18v, 23r, 26v, and 31r; lateral: folio 15v) or lacings (folios 10r, 11r) are even recognizable.

In the preceding 14th century, textile fabrics appear with body armour in a variety of ways. Some of them stand on their own, sometimes a single breastplate is worn over a quilted doublet, sometimes the fabric is used as a cover material over a metal body protection, such as with an early breastplate from the Bayerisches Nationalmuseum (inventory number W 195), or even as a carrier material, as with the brigandine, where numerous overlapping steel plates are riveted to the fabric cover.

It is remarkable that pictures of fighters in armour of the same periode, as for instance with Hans Talhoffer,[51] show the bare metal. On the other hand, the aforementioned fencing master Martin Huntfelt explicitly recommended to cut pieces

46 Augsburg, Universitätsbibliothek, *Cod.I.6.2°.3* and *Cod.I.6.4°.5*, Munich, Bayerische Staatsbibliothek, *Cgm 3711*.

47 Erlangen, Universitätsbibliothek, *B 26*.

48 Munich, Bayerische Staatsbibliothek, *Cgm 1507*; Vienna, Kunsthistorisches Museum, *KK 5126*.

49 Augsburg, Universitätsbibliothek, *Cod.I.6.4°.2*.

50 Gotha, Forschungsbibliothek Schloss Friedenstein, *Ms. Chart. A558*.

51 Gotha, Forschungsbibliothek Schloss Friedenstein, *Ms. Chart. A558*.

from the surcoat of the opponent in order to stab them into his visor with a dagger (Rome, *44 A 8*, folios 92v/93r).

Particularly noteworthy are also the fighters on the left on folios 29r, 34r and 40v, who wear doublets that resemble surviving originals from Lübeck and Stendal: knee-length, padded, quilted tunics with dagged edges, which are attached to the bottom.[52]

The Ecranche

The medieval shield changed continuously over time, just like armour, and was adapted to different needs for the greatest possible protection with unimpeded mobility at the same time. Wood always served as the starting material, and a covering of leather or linen gave the shield further stability. Iron was present only in the form of shield bosses, occasionally as an additional reinforcement of the rim, or as fittings on the surface.[53] The large shields from the 11th century, which tapered towards an acute point at the bottom, and were thus able to protect the entire side of the warrior, became shorter and stockier over time, while the upper, formerly round edge became increasingly flattened: the closed form of the great helm rendered face protection by the shield unnecessary. Over the course of the further development of armour the equestrian shield became less and less important and evolved into a small triangle around the year 1300, called a heater shield. In the late Middle Ages a completely new form of equestrian shield appeared, the convex, outwardly curved, more or less rectangular ecranche—in the German sources known as "tartsche",[54] a term which supposedly derives from the Arabic *dárake* (shield). This could also derive from the Latin *terga* (back), or *tergum tauricum* (oxhide).[55] The Italian *targa* and the English *targe* are related. The origin of the term *ecranche* is somewhat obscure; but the French word *écrancher* essentially means to take the creases out of a cloth. In the older version *écrancer*, the term *cran* referred to a notch.

Once plate armour was fully developed, the shield almost completely lost its relevance and was only used in isolated cases. The Ghent altarpiece by Jan van Eyck,

52 LEHNART: *Kleidung & Waffen der Spätgotik III, 1420–1480*, pp. 126.

53 BOEHEIM: *Handbuch der Waffenkunde*, p. 170.

54 KOHLMORGEN: *Der mittelalterliche Reiterschild*, pp. 130.

55 KOHLMORGEN: *Der mittelalterliche Reiterschild*, p. 131.

dating to 1430, is an example of this. Its panels depict men in harnesses (of the Kastenbrust type) who carry several different forms of ecranche. In the tournament, however, the story is different—until the final decay of the sport, a shield was always in use, and was adapted to the respective discipline.

The time of origin of the *Gladiatoria* manuscripts marked the transition to a complete abandonment of the equestrian shield, which henceforth was used only in the tournament as a *manteau d'armes*, and for the two sportive forms of the joust, called *stechen* and *rennen*.

Ecranches, including those from the *Gladiatoria* group, have an indentation on the right side, the so-called bouche, which served as a means to keep the lance stable on horseback. Thus, these defensive weapons might suggest that the combat on foot was preceded by some fighting on horseback.[56] However, as already mentioned, with a single exception (folio 28r) not even a single fighter has a lance rest, which also allows the lance to be directed more accurately. It is possible that the ecranches were expressly intended for use on foot.

In the Wolfenbüttel *Gladiatoria* version, there are many more techniques than in the other manuscripts of the group; so, for instance, on folios 34r and 37r we see spears inserted into the bouche. Folio 34r (plate 10) is unique among the *Gladiatoria* manuscripts; the ninth technique in the version from New Haven on folio 3v, which corresponds to folio 37r from Wolfenbüttel, shows a different position of the ecranche.

In the New Haven manuscript, the ecranches are utilized only from the ninth to the twelfth techniques of the spear on folios 3v–5r. (The left-hand fighters in the Cracow and Vienna versions refrain from the use of the ecranche in the ninth technique, and in the manuscripts from Cracow and Wolfenbüttel—both of which also contain the first technique of the spear—the left fencer has taken his ecranche loosely in his left hand.) In all other images, the ecranches rest on the floor. None of them allow any heraldic identification of the fighters, but instead uniformly show a red St. George's Cross[57] on a white background. The only other illustrations of armoured

56 In the manuscripts in the tradition of Johannes Liechtenauer, the combat action evolves from the mounted combat with lance and sword towards the dismounted duel with spear, sword and dagger, which can be ended by wrestling or the fight on the ground.

57 St. George was one of the most popular saints of the Middle Ages and a common patron saint particularly for matters of nobility and chivalry. In the fencing books, the St. George's

fighters with ecranches appear in the so-called *Codex Wallerstein*[58] on folios 82v, 88v, 91r, 95v, 103r, 104v, 105r/v, and 107r/v. The armour represented in this manuscript, which is compiled from multiple sources, precedes those from the *Gladiatoria* group (plate 11).[59]

II. ARMS

"It is a constant interaction and reciprocity between arms and body protection that led to new designs and shapes on both sides. As a result, the improvement of one group necessitated the perfection of the other."[60]

Javelin, Spear, and Lance

The spear and the lance were the most widely used weapons of the Middle Ages. Spears and javelins were already used in antiquity. They were about two metres long and thus well suited to be used in a duel in versatile ways. They could either be thrown or used in close combat with one or two hands. The longer lance, which was used on horseback and couched under the arm, appeared in Central Europe in the late 11th or early 12th century. About four meters in length, it was too heavy and too long to find extensive use on foot in the duel.[61] Nevertheless, in the glosses on

---

Cross appears not only as here, in armoured combat, but also as a sign on the big shields for the judicial duel according to Franconian and Swabian law, as we see it with Hans Talhoffer and Paulus Kal. There it appears on both the shields themselves and on the clothing of the fighters (Munich, Bayerische Staatsbibliothek, *Cod. icon 394a*, f. 53v–86r). The duellists in the older part of the Augsburg manuscript *Cod.I.6.402* (*Codex Wallerstein*) also wear surcoats with crosses; however, the colour variations are larger: crosses in red on green, white on red and red on white appear just as frequently as completely monochrome garments.

58 Augsburg, Universitätsbibliothek, *Cod. I.6.4°.2*.

59 In the *Katalog der deutschsprachigen illustrierten Handschriften des Mittelalters*, this part of the manucript is dated to ca. 1420–30 (p. 110)—although this assumption seems to be rather late.

60 Müller/Kunter: *Europäische Helme*, p. 10.

61 Nowakowski: *Arms and Armour in the Medieval Teutonic Order's State in Prussia*. p. 91ff.

Johannes Liechtenauer's verses, the dismounted fighter is still advised to make good use of his lance.[62] The pike however, used in major military formations, could reach even greater lengths of up to six metres.

Occasionally, the precise linguistic definition of the German sources is difficult, so that "Speer" and "Spieß" are often used interchangeably—both of which would translate as "spear". Generally, a "Speer" referred to an appropriate weapon for throwing—a javelin. Boeheim, however, offers a differing definition, calling the staff weapon used on horseback a "Speer"[63]—which goes hand in hand with the bouche in the ecranche that serves to stabilize the spear or lance thrust, and which is called a "Speerruhe" (literally, spear rest) in the old sources. On the other hand, there is the so-called "Rennspieß"—a special tournament lance for the "Rennen" that was three to five metres long. The staff weapon in question, nevertheless, is referred to in the *Gladiatoria* manuscripts as "Spieß" throughout. It could either be thrown or used in close combat.

The length of the spears in the *Gladiatoria* manuscripts seems to be about two to two and a half metres, so they can be considered as too short for use on horseback. The spearheads are kept quite simple; they are double-edged, and the long nozzle is attached to the shaft with a nail.

Numerous *Fechtbücher* describe fencing techniques in harness with the spear; none of the manuscripts that feature only text, however, mention the combined use with the ecranche. The chronologically related manuscripts by Hans Talhoffer[64] also show sword, dagger and spear together in the pictures, but no ecranches.

Illustrated *Fechtbücher* that additionally describe the mounted combat, like those by Paulus Kal,[65] show stylistically very similar spears or lances, whose most obvious difference is the length of the shaft. Interesting in this context are the two images in Kal's *Fechtbücher,* which separate the mounted combat from that on foot; here the dismounted combatant holds the long rider's lance in order to bring the horseman to the ground (plate 12). The next two illustrations show the dismounted harnessed

62 For instance in the codex *44A8*, Rome: Biblioteca dell'Accademia Nazionale dei Lincei e Corsiniana, on f. 54r.

63 BOEHEIM: *Handbuch der Waffenkunde,* p. 305.

64 Particularly the Copenhagen codex *Thott 290 2°* or the Königsegg manuscript *Hs. XIX, 17–3*.

65 Munich, Bayerische Staatsbibliothek, *Cgm 1507* and Vienna, Kunsthistorisches Museum, *KK 5012*.

fighters with shorter spears, followed by another two images with combatants on foot that again use equestrian lances.

In the writings that refer to master Johannes Liechtenauer, the fighting evolves from combat on horseback with lance and sword to dismounted fighting with spear, sword, dagger, and wrestling. It is worth noting in this context that in Paulus Kal's manuscripts, there is also only a single rendition of a harness that is equipped with a lance rest—however, without the depicted lance being inserted.[66]

The Dagger

This short thrusting weapon was mainly suitable for close combat and appears in a plethora of forms. In the present *Gladiatoria* manuscript it occurs almost without exception as a rondel dagger, in which one disc forms the guard and another the pommel. Only in the very first illustration on folio 1r do we see an example of a so-called bollock, bullock, or kidney dagger, characterised by two spherical bulges at the base of the blade. Incidentally, this is the only occurrence of this weapon in the entirety of the manuscripts from the *Gadiatoria* group, although in the artistically less sophisticated Wolfenbüttel version, bollock daggers are possibly also shown on folios 32r, 50v, 68r/v, and 69r/v .

The handles often appear to be studded or ribbed, but the shape of the blades is difficult to identify. Historical dagger blades appear in many different forms: round, one, two, or three-edged or even tetragonal cross sections exist; the blades can have a smooth or ridged surface or can be indented with a variety of fullers.[67]

The dagger was often used as a last resort in armoured combat; once the opponent was taken to the ground or otherwise made unable to move, one should attempt to thrust into the openings of the armour with the dagger to completely persuade the opponent to surrender or even to kill him.[68]

66 Munich: f. 7v, Vienna: f. 11v.

67 Boeheim: *Handbuch der Waffenkunde*, p. 295.

68 See for instance Talhoffer, Königsegg Codex *Hs. XIX*, 17–3, pp. 40–42.

The Sword

The sword was ultimately *the* knightly weapon par excellence, although one can hardly speak of *the* sword. Like armour, the sword changed over the centuries. In the period that concerns us here, it was a versatile weapon that had already undergone a long development. The blades of the swords of the *Gladiatoria* manuscripts taper evenly from the crossguard to the point, the tip of the blade. The quillons are straight or curved only very slightly towards the point; the handle allows the sword to be gripped with both hands; and the generally scent-stopper-shaped pommel is often faceted, with a more or less pronounced sharp chamfered middle edge. Rarely seen is a button or tang nut (e.g. on folio 5v). According to Ewart Oakeshott's sword typology, the illustrated examples correspond to type XVII.[69] These swords, by definition, have a long handle as well as sturdy, long, and slender blades that taper straight to an acute point and provide a hexagonal cross section, sometimes with a shallow fuller.[70]

The plain crossguards belong to Oakeshott type 1 (straight) or 7 (slightly curved towards the blade), the pommels are of type T, T4, or T5.

The handles are depicted rather plainly and do not have a distinct latitudinal ridge or thickening in the middle of the hilt, which appears in several extant specimens and is also commonly found in paintings and sculptures.

Even with this simplicity in terms of the design, the swords nevertheless do not lack the chape, the small leather piece that overlaps the crossguard in a semi-circle over the base of the blade and that is often referred to as a rain guard. However, the assumption that this little piece of leather is supposed to protect the sword against rainwater penetrating into the scabbard appears to be highly doubtful, especially since a sword needs a tight fit in the scabbard to prevent it from falling out in any case, and furthermore the thickness of the crossguard alone should already provide sufficient protection against intruding rainwater. An alternative approach starts from the premise that the toughness of the leather might briefly slow down the opponent's blade as it came sliding along one's own weapon, in order to better protect one's own hand, but might also gain a temporal advantage for counter actions. Another explanation assumes that the copious sweat from the hands, which causes steel to corrode, could be kept away

69 Oakeshott: *Records of the Medieval Sword*, p. 157.
70 Oakeshott: *The Sword in the Age of Chivalry*, p. 65.

from the crossguard and the base of the blade in this way. Since sweat also penetrates leather gloves after a time, such a protective leather piece would be useful both in unarmoured combat as well as in harness. Since the left hand usually precedes the right one in armoured fencing, and thus the opponent's blade hardly can come into contact with one's own crossguard anyway, this explanation seems the most plausible.

Exactly as with armour, the weight of swords is often overestimated. Performances in front of an audience in which faithful replicas are passed around bring forth some estimated weights of five, ten or even fifteen kilogrammes. A second item, presented afterwards for reasons of comparison, a 1.5 litre water bottle, generally evokes some astonishment. On average, one-handed swords weigh 800 grammes to 1.3 kg, two-handed ones 1.4 to 2 kilogrammes, and the large so-called "Bidenhänder" (literally: both-handers) from the Renaissance weigh about 3 kilogrammes.[71] In the appendix to his essay "Anderthalbhänder – Zweihänder – Langes Schwert"[72] Tilmann Wanke mentions the weight of several swords belonging to the same period and of the same type as those from the *Gladiatoria* group. For example cat. no. 5 (hand-and-a-half sword, bastard sword: Collection Fricker, No. 741), weighs 1,250 g at 115 cm; cat. no. 6 (bastard sword, armour-piercing sword: Kunsthistorisches Museum, Vienna, A 168) weighs 1,668 g at 130.2 cm; cat. no. 7 (hand-and-a-half sword: Tower of London, IX 959) weighs 1,250 g at a length of 109.7 cm; cat. no. 15 (two-handed sword: Deutsches Historisches Museum, W 893) weighs 2,190 g at 135.5 cm; cat. no. 16 (bastard sword: Tower of London, IX 16) weighs 1,530 g at 119.4 cm; and finally cat. no. 18 (two-handed sword: Collection Fricker) weighs 1,880 g at a length of 150.9 cm.

One of the most striking techniques is certainly the unscrewing and throwing of the pommel (f. 5r). Beyond the other *Gladiatoria* manuscripts that present the same technique (Cracow: 7r, Vienna: 6r, Wolfenbüttel: 35r), this particular technique appears only in three manuscripts, namely one by Gregor Erhart[73] (folios 217v/218r),[74] one

71 On the subject of sword-physics see also LAIBLE: *Das Schwert*, p. 43ff.

72 WANKE: "Anderthalbhänder – Zweihänder – Langes Schwert", p. 144.

73 Glasgow Museums, R. L. Scott Collection, *E.1939.65.354*.

74 Zewerfen mit dem knopf / Bistu ein starcker man vnd hetest gern end vnd wilt riterliche[n] komen vo[n] aler deiner wer allain vo[n] dem degen so mach dir eine[n] grosen knopf an dein schwert der darab lauft vnd nim dein schwert in die lincken hand beÿ deim gehultz vnd leg es auf den arm vnd dein spies in die rechten hand zu dem schuß vnd den schilt las valen oder nim den spies zu dem schwert als du den zutritzst so nim den knopf vo[n] dem schwert vnd wirf in vnd wen er das weren wil so scheus im zu mit dem spies oder mit dem schwert

attributed to Jörg Wilhalm[75] (fol. 84r)[76] and one by Joachim Meyer[77] (folios 93r/v),[78] although Meyer's version is a little shorter than the other two. Another example, which contains no accompanying text, but rather only an image, can be found on f. 25r of *Cod. 10799* from the Österreichische Nationalbibliothek in Vienna.

This technique is remarkable insofar as the sword was normally constructed in such a way that the tang passed through both the handle and the pommel and was riveted at the end of the pommel, such that it could not easily be taken apart. The modern sporting weapons of foil, epee, and sabre, however, do have removable pommels or handles in order to facilitate quick replacement of a damaged blade.

zwischen zwaien fingern oder halt das schwert weliches du wilt das dir nutz seÿ / bist du der krencker so las in ferwerfen vnd verschiesen das versetz im mit dem schilt vnd arwait mit deiner wer das er nit zu dir kom als ich dich vor gelernet hab. (To throw with the pommel. If you are a strong man, and you want to put an end to it and get rid of your weapons—except the dagger—in a chivalrous way, so have a large pommel made on your sword, which can be removed from it. Take your sword in the left hand by the hilt and put it on your arm. Take your spear in the right hand for the throw and drop your shield, or take the spear together with the sword. If you then step forward, take the pommel off the sword, and cast it. If he wants to ward this off, so throw either the spear or the sword towards him, between two fingers, or keep the sword, just as you like and it may be useful to you. If you are the weaker one, so let him cast or throw. Displace this with the shield and attack with your weapons so that he cannot come to you, as I have taught you before.)

75 Munich, Bayerische Staatsbibliothek, *Cgm 3712*.

76 Zewerffen mit dem knopff
Bistu ein starcker man vnd hetest gernn endt vnd wilt riderlichen komen von aler deiner wer allain von dem degen so mach dir einen grosen knopff an dein schwert der darab lauft vnd nim dein schwert in die linckhen handt beÿ dem gehiltz vnd legs auff dein arm vnd dein spieß in die rechten handt zu dem schus vnd den spies [!] laß falen den spies zu dem schwert als du dem zu drist so nim dein knopff von dem schwert vnd wirff in vnd wen er das weren wil so scheus im zu mit dem spies oder mit dem schwert zwichsen zweÿen fingernn oder halt das schwert welchs du wilt das dir nutz seÿ bistu der krenckher so laß in verwerffen vnd verschiesen das versetz im mit dem schilt vnd arbait mit deiner wer das er nit zu dir kan als Ich dich vor gelernnt hab

77 Rostock, Universitätsbibliothek, *Mss. var. 82*.

78 Bistu ein starck man, vnnd wilt ritterlichen kummen vonn aller deiner wer biß ann degen, mach dir ein großenn knopf an dein Schwert, der da ab lauft, vnnd nim dein schwert in die linckenn handt, beÿ dem gehiltz, vnnd legs auf denn arm, vnnd de[n] Spies in die Rechtenn hanndt, tzu dem schus, vnnd denn schildt las fallenn. Oder nim denn Spies tzu dem schwert, als du dann tzu tritst, so nim denn knopf vom schwert, vnnd wirf im tzu, wen er das weren wil, so scheus im tzu mit dem Spies oder mit dem schwert. Bistu der krencker so las Inn verwerffenn vorschießen, das versetz im mitt dem schilt, vnnd arbeit mit deiner wer, das er nit zu kom, als ich dich vor gelert hab.

Nevertheless, a screwable pommel on a sword is a curiosity and has not survived on any actual weapon according to current knowledge. A closer look at the Talhoffer codex from Copenhagen,[79] however, reveals an illustration of swords for the armoured duel (folio 108r, plate 13): "die zwaÿ swert hörnt zu dem kampf gwauppet." ("These two swords belong to the fight in armour.") One of them possesses a thread, onto the upper end of which a spiky pommel is screwed. This does indeed raise the question of whether there were special swords with removable pommels, particularly designed for the medieval ordeal. In addition to pointed pommels and quillons, Talhoffer also shows spherical bulges in the middle of the blade (plate 14) which might serve to protect the hand, or allow for a firmer grip.

However, the swords depicted in the *Gladiatoria* manuscripts are not exactly like the special swords shown in Hans Talhoffer's aforementioned Copenhagen codex. Furthermore, they don't possess a distinctive ricasso in the middle of the blade as can be seen in a surviving specimen in the Hofjagd- und Rüstkammer in Vienna (cat. no. 6 in Wanke: "Anderthalbhänder – Zweihänder – Langes Schwert").[80] The blade of this remarkable sword has a significant indentation with a distinct rectangular cross section in its middle part, which makes it extremely likely that the sword was supposed to be held specifically in the manner for half-swording techniquess.

In any case, the sword is a multifaceted weapon for a variety of purposes: It can perform strikes and cuts with the edge, the point can be used for thrusting, the crossguard facilitates joint locks and throws, and the pommel can be used as a club for powerful blows. Thus the versatile sword, not to mention all the myths associated with it, is a symbol of chivalry, if not entirely of the Middle Ages and medieval combat.

79 Copenhagen, Det Kongelige Bibliotek, *Thott 290 2°*.

80 Inventory number A 168. Southern Germany, around 1500. Length 123 cm, width 18.5 cm. The *Katalog der Leibrüstkammer, II. Teil* refers to this sword as a "fencing sword", a "type of sporting arm, documented in the fencing literature" (p. 186, fig. p. 96). Nevertheless, this is rather doubtful due to the acute point. The ricasso in the middle of the blade, however, makes it ideal for use in the "armoured hand", i. e. with the left hand in a steel gauntlet grasping the blade.

THE MANUSCRIPT

EDITORIAL GUIDELINES

The text of the transcription on each right-hand page undearneath the image follows the original handwriting as closely as possible. This includes not only word-for-word fidelity, but also punctuation, as well as the use of capital and small initial letters. The punctuation follows the manuscript, though some final sweeps have been omitted; the capitalization closely follows that of the manuscript and even interior capital letters (*gewInnen*) have been retained. When in doubt, we chose a lower-case letter.

Crossed-out or underlined passages have also been retained, and the alignment matches the original. The use of umlauts (particularly *v̈* und *ÿ*) is retained, as well as the richness of variety in Early Modern High German vocabularies (*krafft* and *krefft*, for instance, are used equally and are not adjusted here). Furthermore, the vocalic or consonantic letter *v* has not been adjusted, meaning that a vocalic *v* is not represented by *u*.

We have resolved the numerous abbreviations. To make this clear without impairing readability through an overabundance of brackets, these amendments are set in a shade of grey.

Additions and completions—either those that follow logically from the context, or those that restore lost passages based on the two *Gladiatoria* manuscripts from Cracow and Vienna—are set in square brackets.

The various page, leaf, or technique numberings are left un-transcribed.

In order to facilitate a better understanding of the original sequence of the manuscript, we have decided to offer not only the current folio numbers in large red figures on the top left of each left page, but also the presumed original number in small print in brackets. This foliation follows the assumed reconstructed version that can also be seen in table II on page 239. See also "A Long Time Ago ..." on page 215.

1R (3R)

Note the fourth piece.[1] If he has thrown his spear at you, then grasp your spear with all of your strength, and thrust at him with all force. If he thrusts at you with all of his strength, then strike away[2] his thrust with your left hand, catch it under your left armpit, and hold [it] tight. Take your sword for the throw, and cast [it at] him where you can best reach him.

1 Piece = technique, set of movements.
2 "Striking away" in this sense means defending forcefully.

i *The manuscript starts with the fourth piece; the first three are missing.*

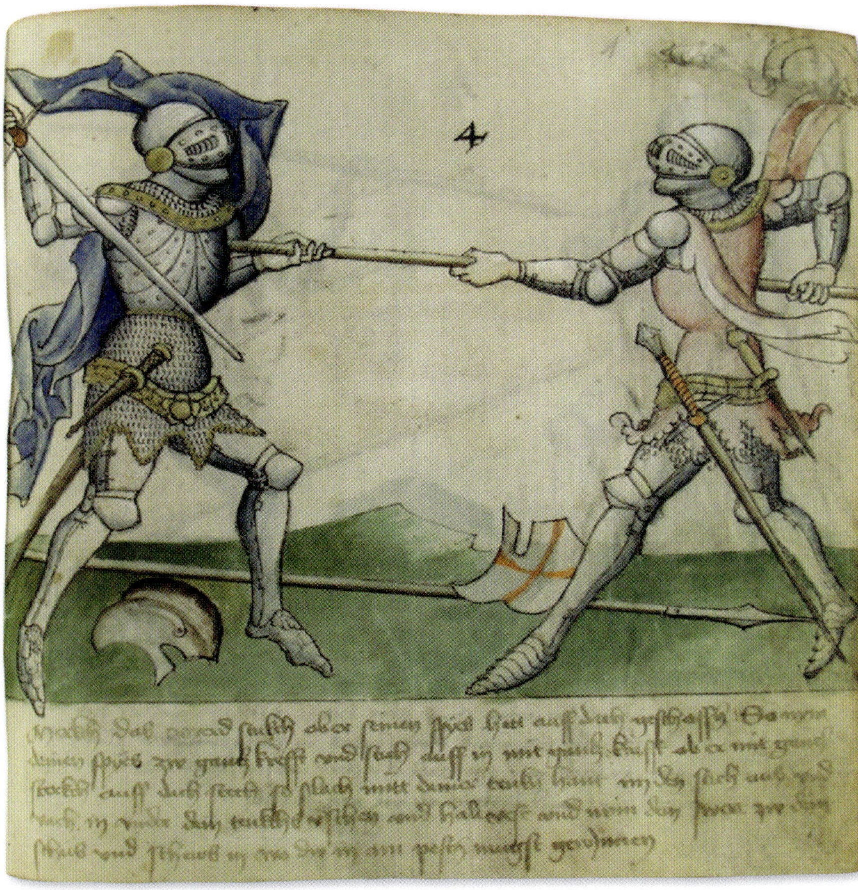

Merckch das vyerd[i] stuckch ober seinen spÿes hett auff dich geschossen So nym deinen spÿes zw gantz krefft vnd stich auff in mit gantz krafft ob er mit gantz sterckch auff dich stech so slach mitt deiner tenken hant im den stich aus vnd vach in vnder dein tenkchs üschen vnd halt vest vnd nim dein swert zw dem schüs vnd schaus in wo dw in am pesten mugst gewInnen

1V (3v)

Note the fifth piece. When you have already thrown your spear, and he attempts to rush[3] at you with his spear, then take your sword in both hands, and strike his thrust away from below and upwards. When you have beaten the thrust aside, then grip your sword in the armoured hand,[4] and work[5] against him with strength.

3 Meaning to beat or attack someone.

4 "Armoured hand" means that only the right hand holds the grip of the sword. The left hand grasps the blade in the middle to put more force and accuracy into the thrust. The hand is "armoured" since these techniques are usually performed in harness, thus the hand is encased in an armoured gauntlet, though in some illustrated fencing books, as in the present one, these gauntlets are not depicted. There are very few exceptions, see fol. 27r and 28v, as well as note xxiv. The reason for this is unclear.

5 Meaning to pressure or attack someone.

ii *Here, "wenn du" is missing not only in this in the manuscript, but also in the Vienna Version (Vienna, Kunsthistorisches Museum,* KK 5013, *subsequently* Gladiatoria *Vienna). Completed according to Cracow, Biblioteka Jagiellońska,* Ms. Germ. Quart. 16 *(subsequently* Gladiatoria *Cracow).*

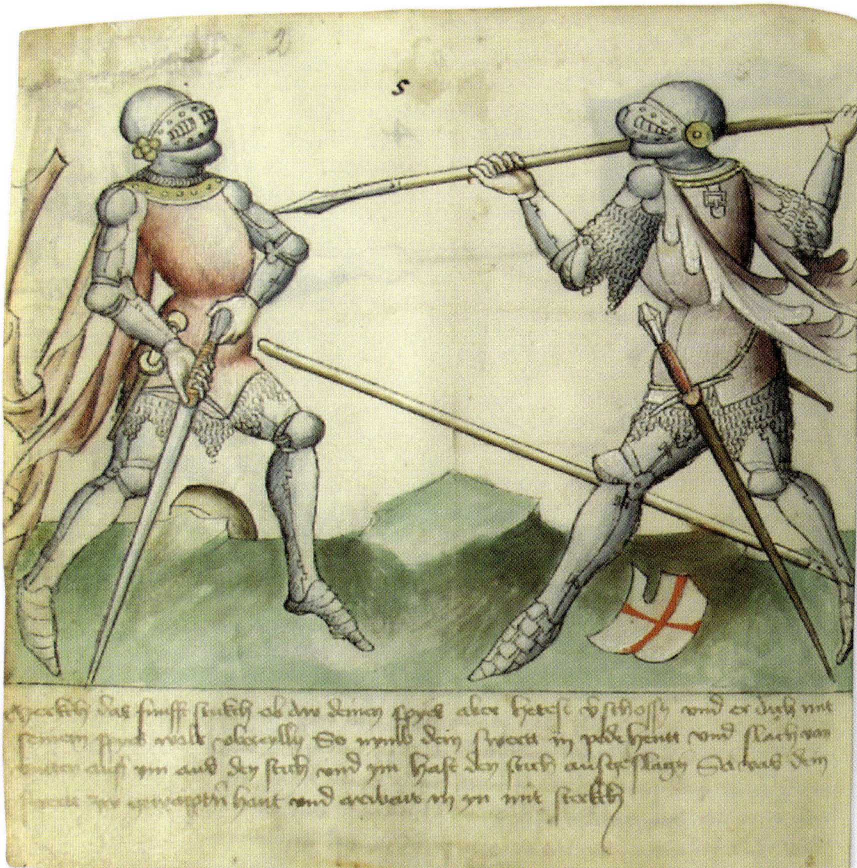

Merkch das funfft stukch ob dw deinen spÿes aber hetest verschossen vnd er dich mit seinem spyes wolt vbereyllen So nymb dein swertt in pede hentt vnd slach von vntten auff ym aus den stich vnd[ii] ym hast den stich ausgeslagen So vas dein swertt zw gewappten hant vnd aribait in yn mit sterkch

Note the sixth piece. If you have thrown your spear at him, and he rushes at you with his thrust so that you can't reach for your sword, then pull out your dagger, and strike his thrust away with your dagger, so that the thrust passes forwards to your left side, and rush at him[6] so that you can rob him of his spear.

6 In this case rushing at someone means quickly seeking body contact with the opponent to conquer him with wrestling techniques.

iii *Recte: "stich" (see* Gladiatoria *Cracow and Vienna).*

Merkch das Sechst stukch ob dw deinen spyes hetst auf in verschossen vnd das er dich mit seinem stich vber eyllett das dw nicht zw deinem swertt machst kömen So czukch aus deinen degenn vnd slach ym den tisch[iii] *aus mit dem degenn das der stich neben der tenken seyttn für gee vnd lauff mit ym ain das dw in auch pringst von dem spyes*

2V (4V)

Note the seventh piece. When you have both lost your spears, and if he can get his sword, and strikes strongly downwards at you, then take your dagger in both hands, and catch the sweeping strike between your two hands on the dagger. Thus you will come to wrestle with him for the sword.

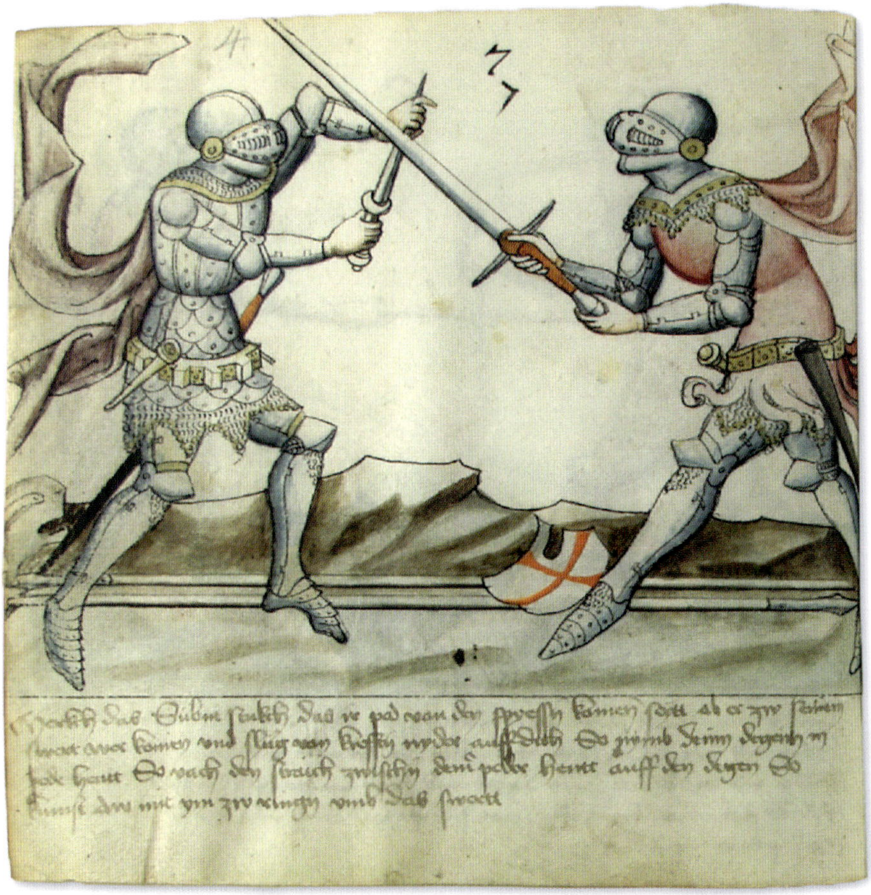

Merkch das Sübnt stukch das ir paid von den spyessen komen seÿtt ob er zw seinem swert wer kömen vnd slüg von krefften nyder auff dich So nÿmb deinn degenn in pede hentt So vach den straich zwischen deiner peder hentt auff den degen So kumst dw mit ym zw ringen vmb das swertt

3R (5R) SPEAR

Note the eighth piece. Then take your spear strongly to throw it, and observe if you can hit him, so that the throw is not made in vain. Now see if he throws [the spear] at you, then grasp your spear strongly for the thrust, watch where you can hit him well, and hold your spear as far in front as you can.

iv *The text portion of this page has been cut off beneath the feet of both fighters. Completed according to* Gladiatoria *Vienna.*

[iv] *[Merkch das acht stukch So nymb deinen spyes mit sterken zw dem schusz vnd merckh ob dw mügest treffn das dw den schuss nicht vmb sunst tüst nw schaw ob er auff dich schüss So nym deinen spyes zw sterckh des stich vnd schaw auff yn wo dw mügest recht treffen vnd halt dich des spyes als lenginst das dw machst]*

3V (5v)

Note the ninth [piece]. When he has taken his ecranche[7] in his left hand, grabbed the spear for the throw, and goes around you and looks where he can hit you well with the throw, then take your spear and ecranche together, put them in front of yourself on the ground, take your sword in your right hand, and wait for the throw that he intends to make at you.

7 A shield with an indentation for the lance, what is referred to as a bouche.

v *The text portion of this page has been cut off beneath the feet of both fighters. Completed according to* Gladiatoria *Vienna.*

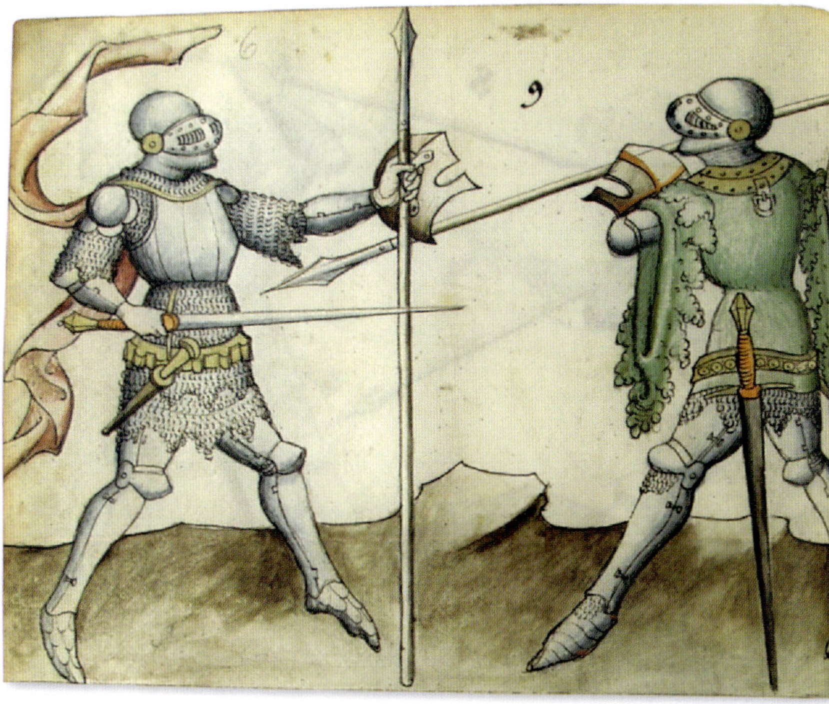

[v] *[Merkch das Newnt ob er sein tarschen hett genamen in sein tenkche hant vnd den spyes hett gevast zw dem schuss vnd gieng vmb dich vnd schawet wo er dich recht an wolt treffn mit dem schuss So nymb deinen spyes vnd tatschen zw sammen vnd setz für dich auff dy erd nym dein swert in dein rechte hant vnd wart auff den schuss den er dir gemaynt hat]*

4R (6R) SPEAR

Note the tenth [piece]. If he has dropped his ecranche, and grasped his spear and sword together, then powerfully thrusts at you with strength, and wants to press at you strongly, then take your spear and ecranche together, set yourself against him fiercely with strength, and keep yourself as far [away] from him as you can.

vi *The text portion of this page has been cut off beneath the feet of both fighters. Completed according to* Gladiatoria *Vienna.*

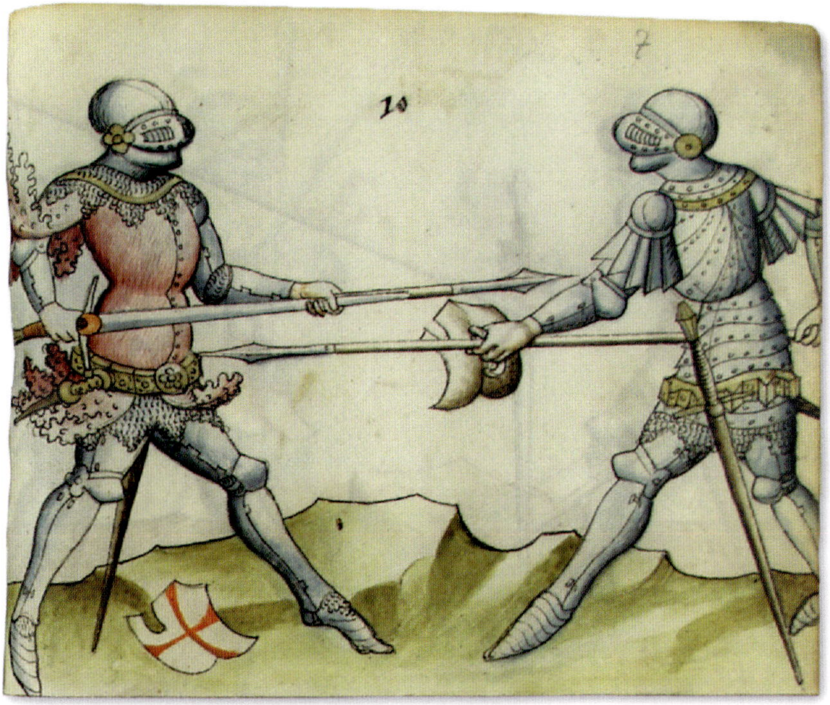

[vi] [Merkch das zehent ob er sein tatschen hett lassen vallen vnd sein spyes vnd swert zw samb gevast hett vnd krefftikleich auff dich stech mit sterkch vnd wolt dich herttikchleichen aribaitten So nymb dein spys vnd tatschen zesamb vnd setz dich hertikchleichen mit sterkch wider in vnd halt dich des als lengist dw machst]

4V (6v) SPEAR

Note the eleventh [piece]. If he has taken his ecranche in his left hand, and brought his spear upwards for the throw, and attempts to throw at you, then take your sword and ecranche together in the left hand, watch carefully for his throw, and catch it on your ecranche. When he has thrown his spear, then jerk your spear upwards for the throw, and immediately throw it at him wherever you can hit him. Thus you will freely come to your sword.

vii *The text portion of this page has been cut off beneath the feet of both fighters. Completed according to* Gladiatoria *Vienna.*

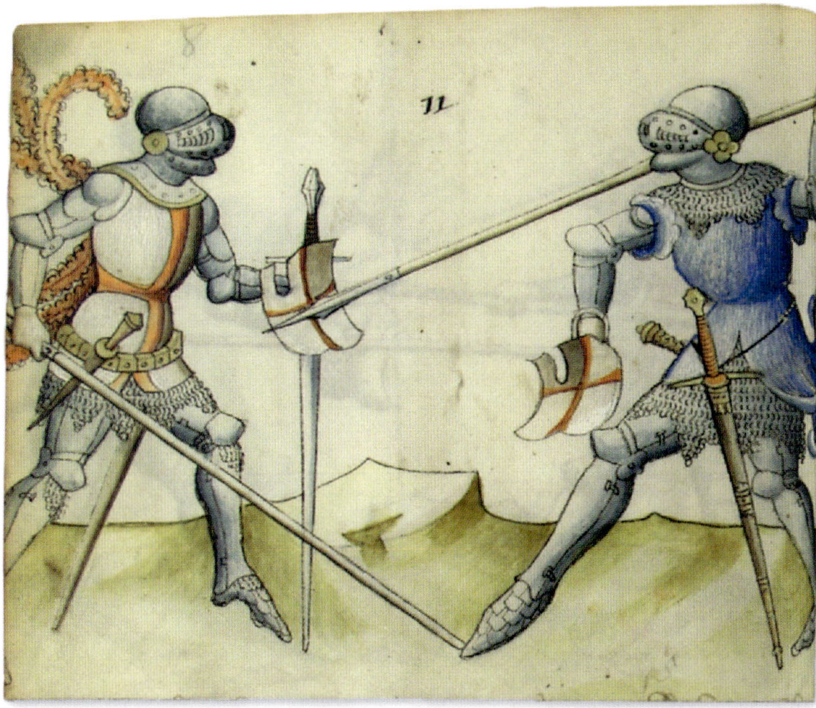

[vii] *[Merkch das Aindlefft ob er seine tatschen hett genomen in sein tenke hant vnd het genomen seinen spyes vbersich auff zw dem schuss vnd wolt dich schiessen So nymb dein swert vnd tatschen zw samb in dye tenkch hant vnd merkch eben auff seinen schus vnd vach den auff dein tatschen wann er seinen spyes verschossen hat so würff deinen spyes vbersich auff zw dem schos vnd scheus fluchs auf in wo dw in treffen kanst So kumst dw frey zw deinem swert]*

Note the twelfth [piece]. If you want to finish him quickly, then take your spear and sword together on your arm, unscrew the pommel from your sword, and throw it at him forcefully. Run at him after the throw, and use the sword or the spear, whichever you consider appropriate. If he throws the pommel at you in this way, then set your ecranche in front of yourself and catch the throw with it. Hold your spear in front of yourself in your right hand, ready to thrust. Protect yourself from him, so he can't run at you as he intends to do.

viii *The word is underlined in pencil.*
ix *Word illegible; completed according to* Gladiatoria *Vienna.*

Merkch das zwelifft ob dw wildt reschleich mit ym entten So nymb deinen spye[s]
vnd swert zw samb an den arm vnd schrawff ab den knöph von deinem swertt
vnd wirff hertikchleichen[viii] *in in vnd lauff nach dem würff mit ym ein vnd [nütz]*[ix]
swert oder spyes welichs dir eben sey ob er also auff dich wurff mit dem knopph
So nym dein taschn für dich vnd vach darauff den wurff vnd nym den spyes
für dich in die recht hant zw dem stich vnd rett dich sein das er dir nicht in lauff
als er yndem synne hatt

5V (7v)

Note the beginning of the short sword.[8] When you have approached your opponent in the lists[9] with all your weapons together – spear, ecranche, sword, and also your dagger – and you have thrown your spear and lost your ecranche, then take your sword in the armoured hand, as you have learnt, and turn[10] it upwards over your head to thrust from above, as you see painted above.

8 The sword itself is not short; only the way of holding it is shortened. It is the same as holding it in the armoured hand (see note 3). This is also called halfsword in other manuscripts.

9 The (wooden) barrier that marks the boundary of the fighting area, for example in an ordeal or judicial duel.

10 Turning (also known as "winding") usually means a turning motion of the sword executed while maintaining contact with the opponent's blade.

x *The text is underlined in pencil.*

Merkch den anefankch des kurczn swertt[x] *vnd wenn dw in die schrenkchn bist kom[en]*
[z]w deinem veint vnd dw alle dein wer peyeinander hast Spies taschen[x] *vnd swert*
vnd auch deinen degen vnd das dw deinen spyes veschossen hast vnd von deiner taschen
komen bist So nymb dein swertt zw gewappten hantt als dw es gelernt hast
vnd wint es vbersich vber dein haupp zw dem stich von oben als dw es oben
gemalt siechst

6R (8R)

Note a piece. When he has raised his sword above himself to thrust, and tries to thrust towards your face with strength, then be alert and thrust with the point of your sword moving upwards from below over his left arm and under his sword, and lift with your point strongly upwards. Thus [you] will tear his hand away from the sword, as you see painted.

Merkch das stukch wenn er hatt sein swert vbersich auff geworffn zw dem Stich vnd wil dir herttikchleichen stechen zw dem gesicht So merkch auf vnd stich von vntten auff mit deinem swertt vber seinen tenkn arm vnder sein swertt mit deinem ortt vnd heb mit deinem ortt vest vbersich So prichst ym dÿ hantt ausdem swertt als dws gemalt siechst

6V (8v)

If he thrusts at you moving upwards from below towards your visor [and] face, and wants to hit you there strongly, then look, grasp your sword short, and watch him closely so that when he strives to thrust at your visor, you hit the inside of his palm with your thrust. Thus you deprive him of his hand, and he will not be able to use it well any more.

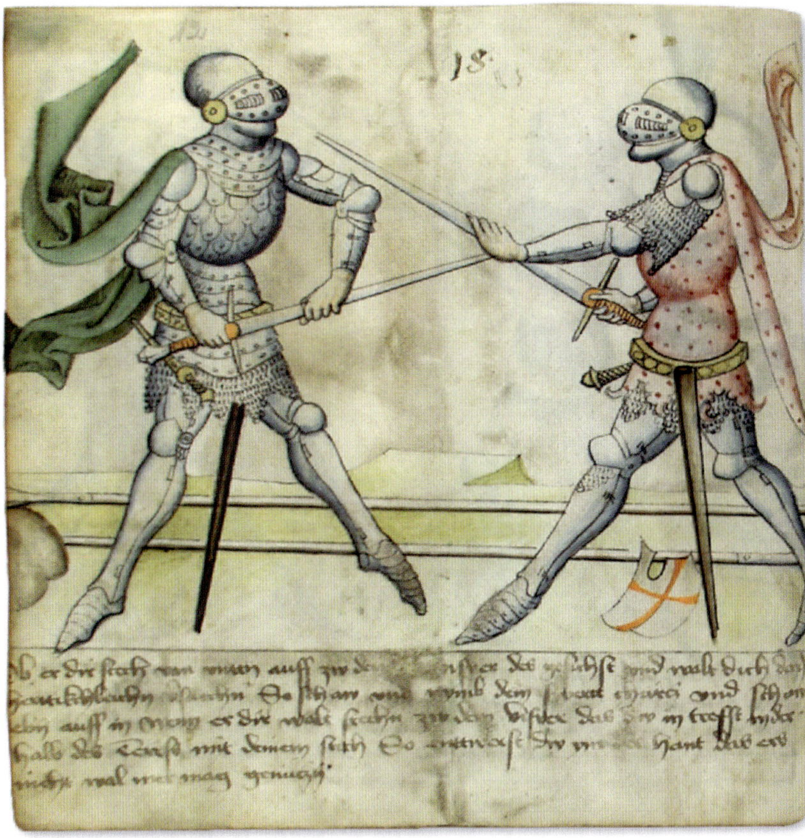

Ob er dir stech von vnttn auff zw de[inem] visyer des gesichst vnd wolt dich darIn herttikchleichn versuechen So schaw vnd nymb dein swertt churcz vnd schaw eben auff in wenn er dir wolt stechn zw dem visyer das dw in trefst inder-halb des Tenrss mit deinem stich So enttwerst dw ym der hant das ers nicht wol mer mag genüczn

7R (12R)

Note a piece, which is called the way of the joints.[11] When both thrust at each other with all of their strength, and you want to execute this piece against him, then thrust from the outside of his sword with the point towards him. Drive your pommel between his two hands, catch him with the pommel over his right hand over the wrist, and pull strongly towards yourself. Thus you will break his arm or throw him, as you see painted above.

11 A singular name that does not occur in any other fencing manuscript. The meaning is not entirely clear. One way of reading may be that we have two consecutive techniques: in the first, the first joint, the wrist, is attacked; in the second, it's the next joint, the elbow.

xi *The text portion of this page has been cut off beneath the feet of both fighters. Completed according to* Gladiatoria *Vienna.*

[xi] *[Merck daz stuck daz man heißet die straß der glider Wann einer gen den anderen stech mit ganczer krafft vnd du daz stuck wilt vf In treiben So stich außerhalb seines swertz mit dem ort gen Im vnd var mit deinen knopf zwischen seiner beider hend durch vnd greif Im mit dem knopf vber sein rechte hant vber daz glid vnd ruck vast an dich So brichst Im den arm oder wirfest In als du es oben gemalet sichst]*

7V (12V)

Note the second piece of the way of the joints. When both thrust at each other, and you want to carry out this piece, then thrust to him yet again outside of his sword, move your pommel between his two hands, catch him with the pommel from the outside over his left arm, and pull strongly towards yourself. Thus you will break his arm or throw him as you see painted above.

xii *The text portion of this page has been cut off beneath the feet of both fighters. Completed according to* Gladiatoria *Vienna.*

[xii] *[Merkch daz ander stukch der straß der glider wan einer aber den vff den andern stech vnd aber daz stukch treiben wil So stich Im aber außerhalb dez swertz vnd var Im durch mit deinem knopf Innerhalb seiner beyder hend vnd greiff Im mit dem knopf außerhalb vber sein tencken arm vnd ruck vast an dich So brichstu Im den arm oder wirfestu In als du es oben gemalt sichst]*

8R (9R) SWORD

If he thrusts at you with all of his strength towards the body from below, then thrust [at] him from above through between his left arm and the sword and lift with the pommel upwards, as you see painted above.

Ob er dir stech mit gancz krafft von vnden auff zw dem leib So stich ym von oben zwischn seins tenkchn arm vnd swert durch vnd heb vbersich mit den knopff als dw es obenn gemalt siechst

8V (9V) SWORD

If you have both thrust towards the face from the inside of each other's swords, then press his point downwards with your sword. With your pommel, go between his left hand and the sword from above and pull strongly towards yourself, as you see painted above.

xiii *Illegible deletion.*

Ob sy bayd ainer den andern ynnerhalb der swertt zw dem gesicht stäch So trib mit dinem [?][xiii] *swertt sein ortt vndersich vnd greyff mit deinem knopph von oben zwischn seiner tenkn hantt vnd Swert durch vnd czukch vast an dich als dw es obn gemalt siechst*

9R (10R) SWORD

If he has put his right foot forwards, and strikes with a murder strike[12] at your head from above, then catch this strike on your sword between your two hands, step with your left foot to the outside of his right foot, and hit his neck from the left side with your point. Thus you will throw him backwards, as you see painted above.

12 A strike with the pommel. See glossary, p. 279.

Ob er den Rechtten fües hett für geseczt vnd slüeg dir obn den mordslag zw dem haubtt So vach den slach zwischn bayder deiner henndt auf dein Swertt vnd schraÿtt mit deinem tenckn fues ausserhalb seins Rechttn fües vnd greyff mit deinem ortt an seinen hals zw der tenken seytten So wirffestu ym vber rukch als dw es oben gemalt siechst

If he has put his left foot forwards, and strikes at your head with the murder strike from above, then catch this strike on your sword between your two hands. Step forwards to the outside of his left foot with your right foot, and catch his neck with your pommel on the right side. Thus you will throw him backwards, as you see painted above.

Ob er seynn tenken fües hett fürgesecztt vnd slueg dir von obn den mordslag zw
dem hawpph So vach den slag zwischen bayd deiner hennde auff dein Swertt So
schraÿtt für mit deinem rechten fues ausserhalb seins tenken fues vnd greyff
mit deinem knopph zw seinem hals an der rechten seytten So wirffestu ÿm zw
[ru]kch als dw es obn gemalt siechst

10R (11R) SWORD

If he has turned his pommel forwards, and strives to shatter your left arm between the elbow and shoulder, then throw your sword forwards to the side, and turn your point upwards. Thus you have parried the strike, as you see painted above.

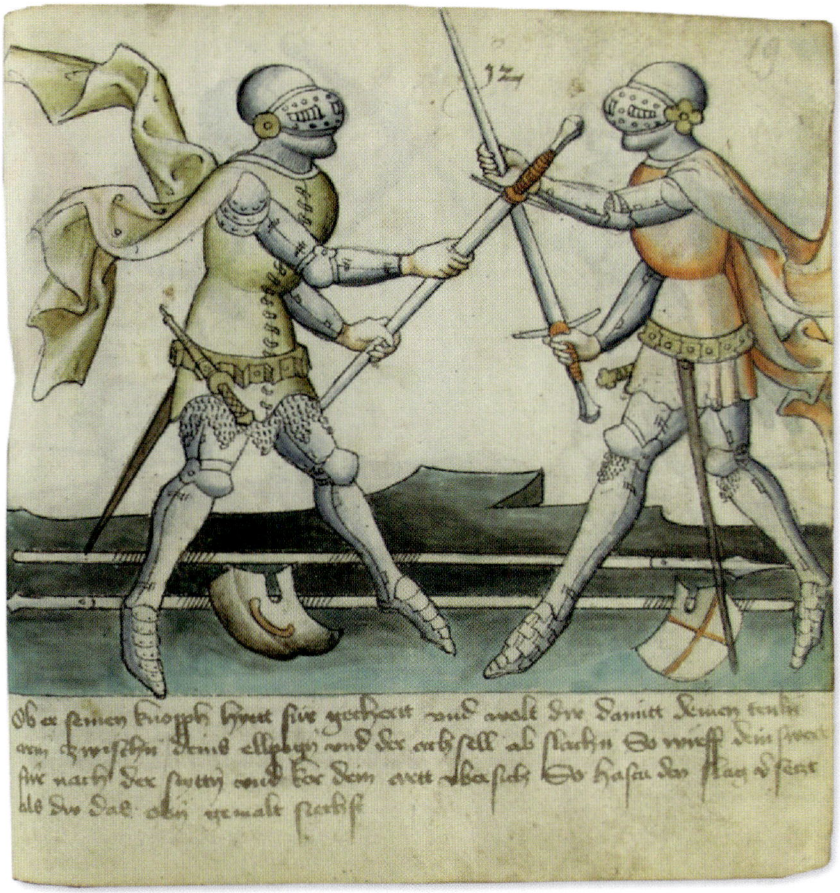

Ob er seinen knopph hyett für gechertt vnd wolt dir damitt deinen tenken arm zwischen deins ellpogen vnd der achsell ab slachn So wirff dein swert für nach der seytten vnd ker dein ortt vbersich So hastu den slag verseczt als dw das oben gemalt siechst

10V (11V)

If he has turned his pommel forwards, and strives to shatter your right arm between the elbow and shoulder with it, then throw your sword forwards to the side, and turn your point upwards as well. Thus you have blocked his strike, as you see painted above.

Ob er hett seinen knopph für gekertt vnd wolt dir damitt deinen rechten arm zwischen deins ellpogens vnd der achsell ab slachen So wirff dein swert für nach der seytten vnd ker dein ortt aber vbersich So hastu den slag verseczt als dw es oben gemalt siechst

11R (13R) SWORD

When you thrust towards his face inside of his sword, then grasp his left hand behind the wrist with your left hand on your sword. Step inside his left foot with your right foot, and lift his arm upwards with your sword. Thus you will throw him forwards, as you see painted above.

Wenn dw Im stichst ynnerhalb seins swerts zw den gesicht So nÿmb sein tenke hantt hinder den glid mit deiner tenken hantt zw deinem swertt vnd schraitt mit deinem rechten fues Innerhalb seins tenken fues vnd heb ym mit deinem swertt seinen arm vbersich So wirffestu Im fürsich als dw es obn gemalt siechst

11V (13v)

This is the break.[13] Take note: grasp his left side under his left arm with your left arm, grasp his right knee-bend with your right hand from the outside, and lift upwards. Thus you will throw him on his back, as you see painted above.

13 A counter against a piece.

Das ist der prüch nw merkch greyff mit deinem tenken arm in seine tenke syt[en] vnder seinen tenken arm vnd greyff mit deiner rechten hant auswendig in sein rechte knyepüg vnd heb vbersich So wirffestw im auff den Rukch als dw es oben gemalt siechst

12R (14R)

When you again thrust at his face inside his sword, grab his left hand behind the wrist with your left hand on your sword, step with your left foot inside his left foot, and lift his arm upwards with your sword. When you have brought him to this point, then let your left hand leave the sword and quickly grasp over his neck. With your right hand grasp his left thigh from the inside. Thus you will throw him away from yourself, as you see painted above.

Wenn dw ym aber stichst Innerhalb seins swert zw dem gesicht So nym se[in]
tenke hantt hinder den glid mit deiner tenken hantt zw deinem swert vnd schrai[tt]
mit deinem tenken fues ynnerhalb seins tenken fües vnd heb mit deinem swertt
seinen arm vbersich wann dw in darzw pracht hast So la varn die tenke
hant aus dem swertt vnd greyff ym damit reschleich vber den hals vnd mit
deiner rechten hant vass sein tenks diech Innerhalb So wirffestu in von dir
als dw oben gemalt siechst

12V (14V) SWORD

Grasp over his back and under his right armpit with your left arm, and his left thigh from the outside with your right. Pull strongly towards yourself. Thus you will throw him to the ground in front of you, as you see painted above.

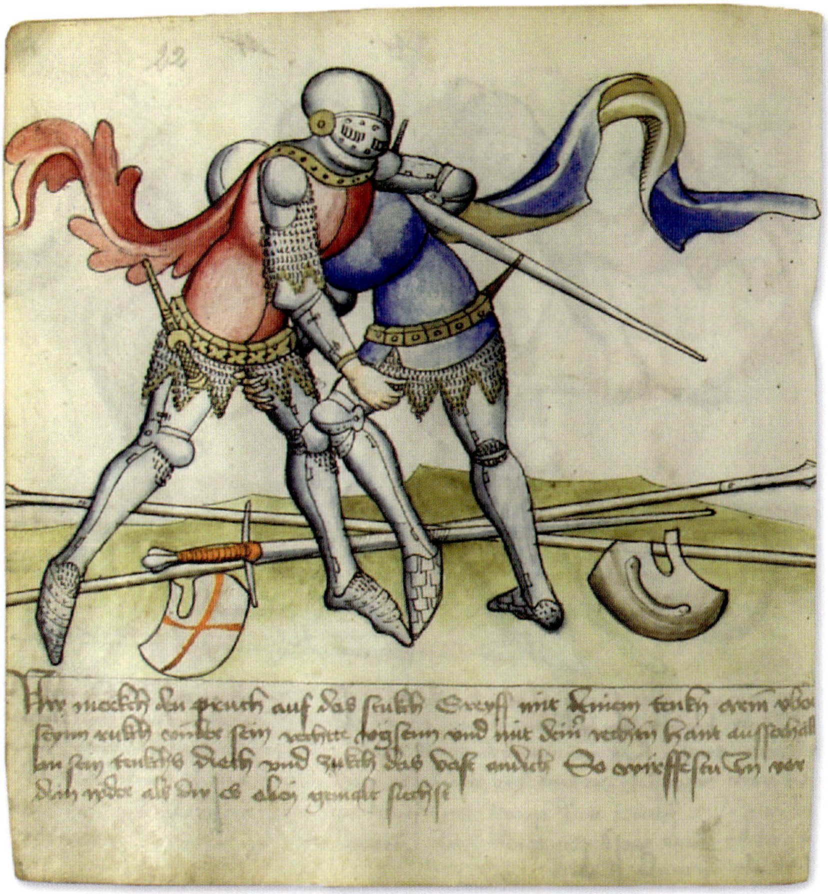

Nw merkch den pruch auf das stukch Greyff mit deinem tenken armm vber seynn rukch vnder sein rechtte vgsenn vnd mit deiner rechten hant ausserhalb an sein tenkchs diech vnd zukch das vast andich So wirffestu In vor dein nyder als dw es oben gemalt siechst

13R (15R) SWORD

Perform this piece that you know well to conquer his back with. Then lift him straight upwards, strike him with your left knee to the outside of his left knee, and swing him down in front of yourself, as you see painted above.

Das stukch nÿmb für dich als dw wol waist damit dw Im angewInnst sein ruken So heb In gerad vbersich auff vnd slach vnd slach [!] ym mitt deinem tenkn knÿe ausserhalb an sein tenks chnÿe vnd swing In fur dich nyder als dw es oben gemalt siechst

13V (15V) SWORD

Note the piece. When both of you have thrust strongly at each other towards the body, then grasp his left hand at the wrist and both swords together in your left hand, go through with your pommel under his right arm, and jerk strongly upwards. Thus you have taken his sword, as you see painted above.

Merkch das stukch wenn es bayd stecht mit krafft Zu dem leib So nym sein [t]enke hant bey dem glid vnd bayde swertt zw samb in dein tenke hant var [i]m mit deinem knopph ünder seinen rechten arm durch vnd rukch vast vber sich So hastu ym sein swert enttwert als dw es oben gemalt sichst

14R (16R)

Note the break. Take both points in your left hand, and jerk strongly towards your left side. Grasp him with your left hand over his back, under his right armpit and grasp his left thigh from the outside with your right hand. Throw him in front of yourself, as you see painted above.

Mer den pruch nym bayde ortt in dein tenke hantt vnd rukch vast an de[in] tenke seytten vnd greyff mit deiner tenken hant vber seinen ruken vnder seine rechtt vgsen vnd greyff mit deiner rechten hant ausserhalb an sein tenkchs diech vnd wirff in von dir als dw es oben gemalt siechst

14V (16v)

Note the counter-break. Catch him around his whole body with your left arm. Pull him strongly towards yourself, grab his left knee with your right hand. Throw him with a wrestling technique as you see painted above.

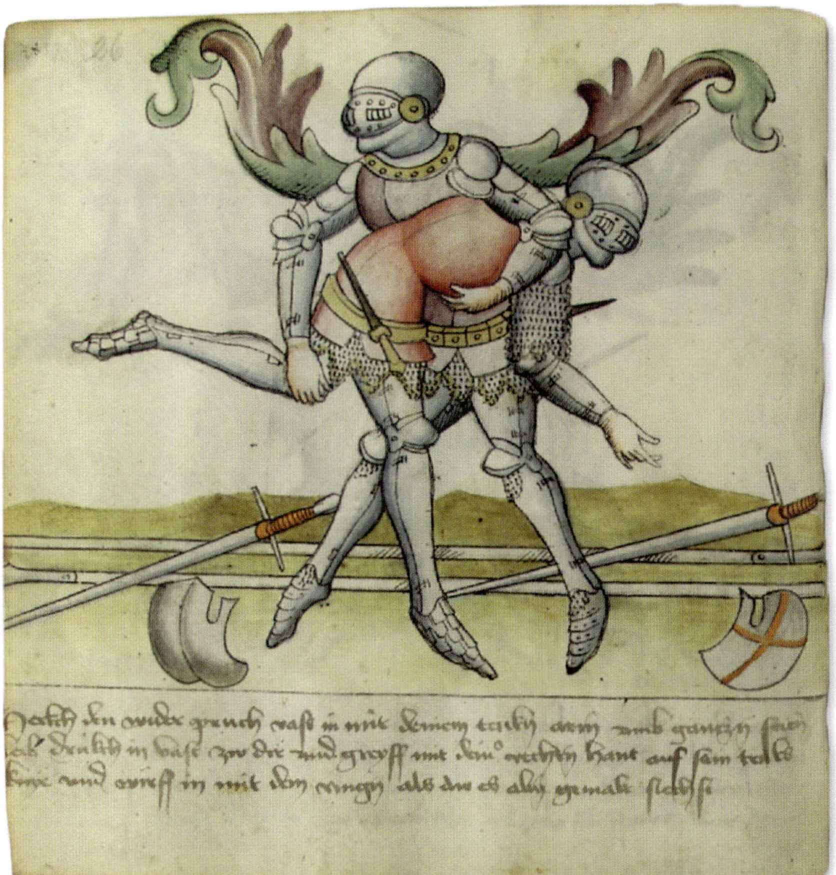

Merkch den wider pruch vass in mit deinem tenkn arm vmb ganczn seien leib drukch in vast zw dir vnd greyff mit deiner rechten hant auf sein tenks knÿe vnd wirff in mit dem ringn als dw es oben gemalt siechst

15R (21R) SWORD

Note the piece: the beginning of the scissors. If one has grasped the other one's sword by the point, then throw yourself to the other side of the swords, as you well know. In this way you will free your sword from him. Hold his point still and thrust with your sword over his grip inside his right elbow. Lift upwards, and thus you will deprive him of his sword, as you see painted above.

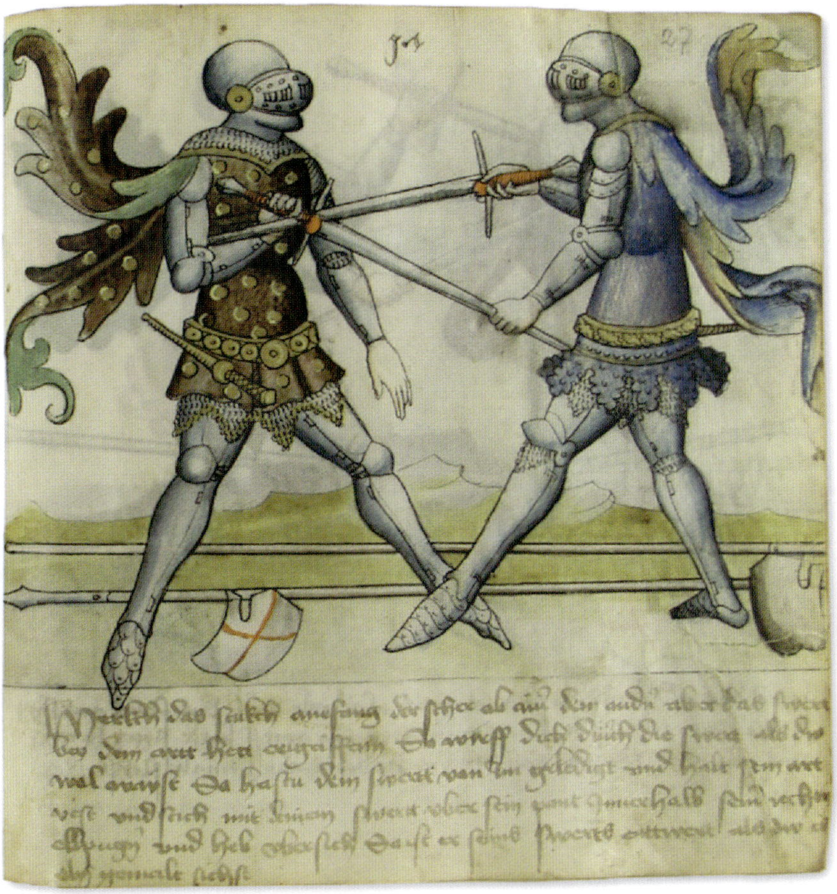

Merkch das stukch anefang der scher ob ainer dem andern aber das swert bey dem ortt hett ergriffenn So wirff dich durch die swert als dw wol waÿst So hastu dein swertt von Im geledigt vnd halt sein ort vest vnd stich mit deinem swertt vber sin pant Innerhalb seins rechtn ellpugn vnd heb vbersich So ist er seins swerts enttwert als dw es oben gemalt sichst

15V (21V) SWORD

Note the second piece of the scissors. If he attempts to throw himself to the other side of the sword, then watch for the moment when he turns his back to you. Then throw both swords crosswise over him, and keep him close to yourself, as you see it painted above.

Merkch das ander stukch der scher ob er sich aber wolt durch das swert werffn
So schaw als pald er dir deinen ruken chertt So wirff beyde swert krewts
weis vber in vnd halt in vest zw dir als dw es obn gemalt sichst

16R (22R) SWORD

Note a break against both pieces of the scissors. If he has thrown both swords over you, then drop your sword. Grasp the blade of his sword with your left hand and his handle above his hand with the right hand. Thus you have lost your sword, and taken his, as you see painted above.

Merkch den pruch bayder Stukch der schër ob er waid swert vber dich gew[orffen]
hett So lasse valln dein Swert vnd greyff mit deiner tenkn hant In sein s[werts]
chlingen vnd mit deiner rechten hant ob seiner hant In das pant So bistu [von]
deinem swert komen vnd hast Im das sein genomen als dw es oben gema[lt]
siechst

16V (22V)

Note the piece. If you have both thrust at each other from the outside of the swords towards the face, and [he] attempted to turn your point away, then push strongly away from yourself with the point. Let go of the sword with your left hand, grasp his pommel with it, and lift upwards. Thus you will turn him away from yourself so that he turns his back to you, as you see painted above.

Merkch das Stukch ob ir bayd ainer den andern het gestochen ausserhalben des [s]werts zw dem gesicht vnd dein ort aus hett welln wennden So drukch vast [v]on dir mit deinem ortt vnd lass varen dein tenke hant aus dem swert vnd greyff damit nach seinem ~~swert~~ knopff vnd heb vber sich So wenndestw in von dir das er dir kertt den rukch als dw es oben gemalt sichst

17R (23R) SWORD

Note a break. Let go of the sword as soon as he has grasped the pommel, and hit his arm behind his left elbow with it. Thus you will do to him what he wanted to do to you, as you see painted above.

Merkch den pruch als er dir nach dem knopff hatt griffenn So lass varn dein rechtte hant aus dem swert vnd stoos in damit hinder seinen tenckn ellpogen an dem arm So pringstu in darzw als er dir vor hett wellen tün als dw es oben gemalt siechst

17V (23V)

Note the piece. If both swords meet when thrusting to the face from the outside, then catch the hollow of his left knee with your pommel from the outside. Pull strongly towards yourself, and hit him with your left elbow at his breast. Thus you will throw him backwards away from yourself, as you see it painted above.

Merkch das stukch ob bayde swertt mit dem stich ausserhalb begegent an ain ander zw dem gesicht So greyff mit deinem knopff ausserhalb sein tenkch knyepug vnd rukch vast an dich vnd stoos in mit deinem tenkn ellpogenn in sein prust So wirffestu in von dir vber rukch als dw es oben gemalt sichst

18R (24R) SWORD

Note the break. Drop your sword and grasp over the neck at his right shoulder with your left hand. With your right hand, grasp his left thigh from the outside and jerk him upwards. Thus you will throw him down, as you see it painted above.

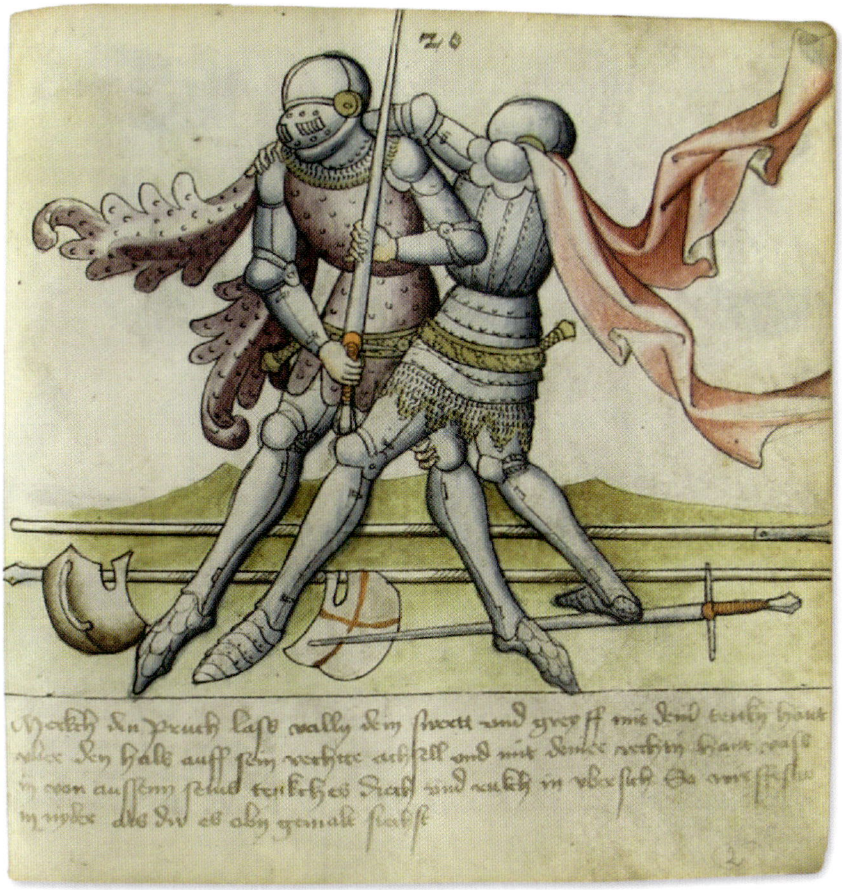

Merkch den Pruch lass valln dein swertt vnd greyff mit deiner tenken hant vber den hals auff sein rechtte achsell vnd mit deiner rechten hant vass in von aussenn seins tenkches diech vnd rukch in vbersich So wirffestw in nyder als dw es obn gemalt siechst

18V (24V)

Note the piece. If both have thrust at each other inside the swords towards the body, then push his point downwards with your sword and catch the hollow of his left knee with the pommel. Pull strongly towards yourself and hit him in his left armpit with your head. Thus you will throw him backwards, as you see painted above.

Merkch das stukch ob aine den anden hett gestochenn Innerhalb des swerts In den leib So drukch mit deinem swertt sein ort nyder vnd greyff mit dem knopff in sein tenke chnye püg vnd rukch vast andich vnd stos in mit deinem haupp in sein tenke ~~chnyepug~~ vgsenn So wirffestu in vber rukch als dw es obenn gemalt siechst

19R (28R)

Note the piece. If both have thrust at each other strongly towards the breast in such a way that both swords came together on the outside of the bodies, then lift his point strongly upwards with your sword, lift your left foot, and dislocate his leg at the knee, as you see painted above.

xiv *The word "tencken" is missing here. (See* Gladiatoria *Vienna and Cracow.)*

Merkch das Stukch ob ainer den andern herttikchleich hett gestochenn zw [der] prüst vnd das die Swertt ausserhalb der leib aneinander wern komen So [heb] mit deym swertt sein ortt starkch vbersich auff vnd heb auff deynn[xiv] *fues vnd st[os] ym ab sein pain in dem knÿe als dw es obn gemalt siechst*

19V (28v)

Note the break. When he attempts to break your left leg with his foot, then pull this foot backwards, step in front of his left foot to the outside with your right foot and catch the right side of his neck with the pommel. Thus you will throw him on his back away from you, as you see painted above.

xv *"dein" in* Gladiatoria *Cracow. In* Gladiatoria *Vienna it also says "sein".*

Merkch den pruch als er dir mit seinem füs hatt wellenn abstossenn sein[xv] tenks
[p]ain So czukch den selbn füs hindersich Schreytt mit deinem rechten fües aussn
[fü]r seinen tenken fuessen vnd greyff in mit dem knopff zw der rechten seytten seins
hals So wirffestu in von dir an den rukn als dw es oben gemalt siechst

20R (29v)

Note the wrestling piece of the scales. When you have both thrust towards each other's faces from the outside of your swords, then let your right hand leave the sword, and hit him with it at his left arm behind his elbow. Step with your right foot behind his left foot, and move with your right arm strongly around his body. Thus you will throw him, as you see painted above.

xvi *"innerhalb" in* Gladiatoria *Cracow.*

Merkch das stukch des ringen aus der wag wenn Si waid zw ein ander stechn ausserhalb[xvi] der swertt zu dem gesichtt lass varen dein rechtte hantt aus dem swertt vnd stoos in damitt an seynn tenkn arm hinder den ellpogn vnd schreit mit deinem rechten fües für seinen tenkn fues rukchalben vnd var resc[h] mit deinem rechtn arm vmb seinen leib So wirffestu in als dw es obn gema[lt] sichst

20V (29R)

Note the piece. If you have come together and begun wrestling, having both lost all your weapons, and he has now quickly recovered his sword, steps forward with his right foot, and strives to strike your down with all of his strength, then put your left foot forwards, and lay your left arm over your right arm. Catch the strike on your two arms in front of the elbows, and grasp his neck with your left hand [...]

xvii *Curiously this is the description of a break against a piece which is written underneath the same image in both* Gladiatoria *Cracow and Vienna (completed according to the Vienna version):* *"Merkch daz stuck ob du In hast bracht von aller seiner wer von dem Spieß tarzschen Swert vnd degen So ker fur deinen knopf des Swertz vnd slag mit ganczer sterck vff In wo du In weist am herttisten ze treffen da mit daz du In mogst pringen zu der erden"*
(Note the piece. When you have taken all of his weapons—spear, ecranche, sword and dagger, then turn the pommel of your sword forward and strike him with all of your strength where you think you can hit him most forcefully. With this, you may take him to the ground.)

xviii *The rest of the line vanishes in the cut-off area.*

[xvii] *Merkch das Stukch als es ped mit ringen zw sammen kumen seytt vnd daz ainer den andern gar von seiner wer pracht hatt ob er nw reschleich wider komen wër zw seinem swert vnd für schritt mit seinem rechten fues vnd wolt dich mit ganczer krafft slachen darnyder So secz deinen tenken fues für vnd leg deinen tenkn arm auff deinen rechten arm vnd vach den straich auff pede dein arm vor des ellpogns vnd greyff mit deiner tenken hant Im seinen hals*[xviii]

21R (30R) WRESTLING

Note a wrestling piece. When you have both lost your weapons, and grabbed each other to wrestle by the arms, and both hold each other strongly, then try to strike his arm away with strength. If he holds tight and will not let it go, then move your right arm to the side of his thumb. Strike the inside of his elbow and quickly grasp his left hand with yours. In this way, you will force it behind his back. Step in front of him with your right foot. In this way, you will throw him as you see painted above.

xix *Due to the clipping parts of the text are illegible. Completed according to* Gladiatoria *Vienna.*

Merkch das stukch des ringn als sy baid seÿnn komen von der wer vnd zw ein ander greyffenn ze ringn aus dem arm vnd ainer den andern vestikchleich hat gevast So versüch mit sterkch aus ze slachen seÿnn arm hat er vest vnd wil nicht lassen So var mit deinem rechten arm dawmen halbn durch vnd stos [im] den ellpogn einwerts vnd greyff resch mit deiner tenken hant nach seiner tenken h[ant] So nöttstu Ims hinder den rugk vnd schreyt mit deiem rechtn fus für in S[o wirffestu In als du es oben gemalet sichst][xix]

21V (30v)

Note this, another wrestling piece. When he has grabbed his sword again, hurry and prevent him from grasping it with both hands. If he throws his left hand forwards, and thrusts towards your breast, and tries to prevent you from coming towards him, then quickly grasp his left hand with your right hand, and step forward. Step forward with your head under his armpit and your left arm around his body below. Thus you will throw him over your back on his head, as you see painted above.

xx *Some words are illegible because of the clipping. Completed according to* Gladiatoria *Vienna.*

Merkch aber ain stukch von Ringen das er wider hatt pegriffenn sein
Swertt so eÿll resch das ers nicht wegreyff in sein bayd henndt ob
er die tenkch hant für würff vnd stiess dich in dein prust vnd wolt
dich nicht In Im lassen So greyff mit deiner rechten hant resch nach
seiner tenkn hant vnd schreytt für vnd var Im durch sein tenke ~~seyttn~~
vgsen mit dein haupp vnd mit dein tenken arm vnden vmb den leib So
wirffstu In vber deinen rukch [auf sein haubt][xx] als dw es oben gemalt sichst

22R (27R)

Note the break. When he attempts to grab you, jerk your left foot towards yourself and grab him in the same manner he attempted to grab you. Drop your sword, and grasp him by his left thigh. Thus you will throw him to the ground away from you, as you see painted above.

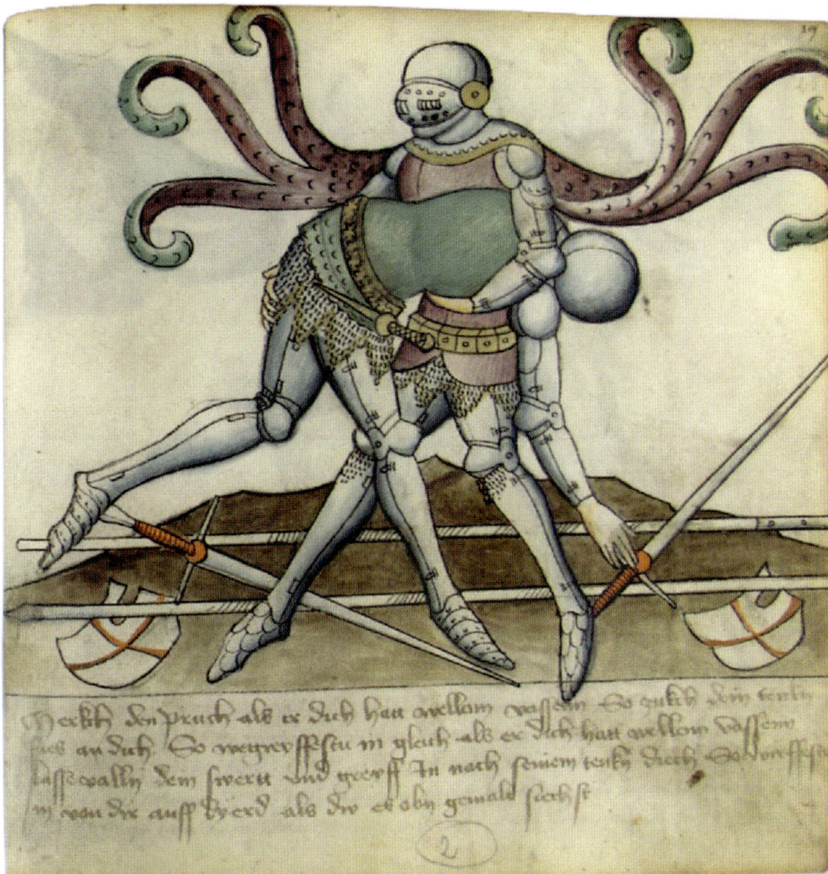

Merkch den pruch als er dich hatt wellenn vassenn So zukch dein tenkn fues an dich So wegreyffestu in gleich als er dich hatt wellenn vassenn lasse valln dein swertt vnd greyff In nach seinem tenkn diech So wirffestu in von dir auff dÿ erd als dw es obn gemalt siechst

22V (27V)

Note the piece. When you thrust towards his face from the inside of the sword and he strives to parry it, then push his sword downward with your point. Thrust your sword towards his neck and let go of the sword with your left hand. Reach around his neck and grasp your sword's grip again on his right side. Thus you have confined him. Thrust with your dagger as you see painted above.

Merkch das stukch wann dw in Innerhalb des Swerts stichst zu dem gesicht
ob er dir den stich wolt verseczen So drukch mit deinem ortt sein Swertt vndersich
vnd stos mit deinem swertt an den hals vnd la varen dein tenke hant aus dem
swertt greyff Im zw der rechtenn seyttenn vmb den hals wider in dein pant
So hastu yn geslossenn vnd stich mit dein degenn als dw es oben gemalt sichst

23R (17R)

Note the piece. When both of you have strongly thrust towards each other's faces outside of the swords, and he attempts to push your point away with strength, then let your point go and step behind his left foot with your right foot. Hit his neck with your sword between your two hands. Thus he will fall, as you see painted above.

Merkch das stukch wenn ainer dem andnern ausserhalb der swert zw dem ges[icht]
sticht vnd dein ortt mit sterkch welle austreiben So lass nach dem ort vnd
schraytt mit deinem rechten fues hinder seinen tenkn fües vnd stos mit d[einem]
swertt zwischen bayder deiner hentt Im an den hals So vellt er als dw es o[ben]
gemalt siechst

23V (17V)

Note a piece. If each of you has set your point on the other's breast, then do not forget the work[14] that comes from it, which you know well and is painted hereafter.

14 Further attacks and pieces, see note 5.

Merkch das stukch wenn ainer dem andern das ortt an die brusst hat gesecztt
[ver]gis nicht der aribaitt die daraus gett als dw wol waist vnd hernach
[ge]malt ist

24R (19R)

Note the break. If he has turned you away from himself with his sword, then grasp him about his neck with your left arm. Grasp him under his right armpit with your hand and drop your sword. Grasp his left thigh from the outside with your right hand and lift upwards. Thus you will throw him, as you see painted above.

Merkch den pruch ob er dich hett geriden von Im mit seÿm swertt So greyff mit deinem tenken arm vber seynn hals vnd vass in mit deiner hant vnder sein[en] rechtn vgsen vnd lass vallen dein swertt vnd greyff mit deiner rechten hantt von aussen in sein tenkes diech vnd heb vbersich So wirffestu in als dw es obn gemalt siechst

24V (19v)

Note the piece. When you have both thrust at each other's body from the outside of the swords, let go of the sword with your left hand. Move your sword under his right armpit and quickly grasp the point again. Lift up, and you will force him to fall, as you see painted above.

Merkch das stukch wenn ir stecht ausserhalb der swertt zw ganczn leib
So la varn dein tenke hantt aus deinem swertt vnd küm ym durch mit
deinem swertt durch seinem rechte ügsen vnd greyff reschleich wider
nach deinem ortt vnd heb vber sich So nottestu In zw dem vall als
dw es oben gemalt sichst

25R (20R)

Note the break. Turn forcefully as soon as he has thrust under your armpit. Throw your sword towards the left side of his neck so his head is between the sword and your arm. Pull him down to the ground, as you see painted above.

xxi *"nyder" in* Gladiatoria *Vienna.*

Merkch den pruch als er dir hatt gestochen durch dein vgsen So czukch di[ch]
vmb mit chrefften vnd wirff ÿm dein swertt ze der tenkchen seytten an d[en]
hals damit sein haubt kom zwischn swertt vnd deins arms vnd rukc[h]
in wider[xxi] zw der erden als dw es obn gemalt sichst

25V (20V)

This piece also belongs to the pressing[15] on the breast. When you both have grasped each other's point in your hands, then jerk your sword strongly towards yourself. If he strives not to yield it to you, then throw the pommel at his right side. Grasp his left knee from the outside with your left hand. Pull towards yourself and strike his left shoulder with your right hand. Thus you will throw him, as you see painted above.

15 A situation in which both opponents have set their points onto the adversary's chest, occasionally also referred to as "gedreng".

Das stukch ist auch von dem dringen an die prust komen das ainer dem andern sein ortt hatt ergriffenn in die hant So zukch dein swert vast an dich wil er dirs nicht lassen So wirff ym deinen knoph in sein rechte seyttn vnd greyff mit deiner tenken hant aussen an sein tenkchs knye rukch an dich vnd stoos mit deiner rechtn hant auff sein tenke achsell So wirfestu in als dw es oben gemalt sichst

26R (18R) SWORD

When you have both pressed your points against each other's chests, then grasp his left wrist with your left hand. Push him away from you with your point so that you can bring his point under your left armpit. Then thrust your sword against his foot, as you see painted above.

xxii *A passage is missing here, completed according to* Gladiatoria *Vienna: "an das glid seiner tenken hant".*

Wenn es mit sterkch an die prüst mit den örtern habt gedrungen So greyff mit deiner tenkn hant[xxii] *vnd stoos in mit deinem ortt von dir damitt dw sein ortt vnder dein tenkche ügsen pringest So stich In mit deim swert in sein fües als dw es oben gemalt siechst*

26V (18v)

Take careful note of this piece. If you attempt to strike the outside of his left knee with your pommel and he notices this and attempts to parry the strike, then hold fast and thrust through from the outside of his sword under his left leg. Turn him away from you, as you see painted above.

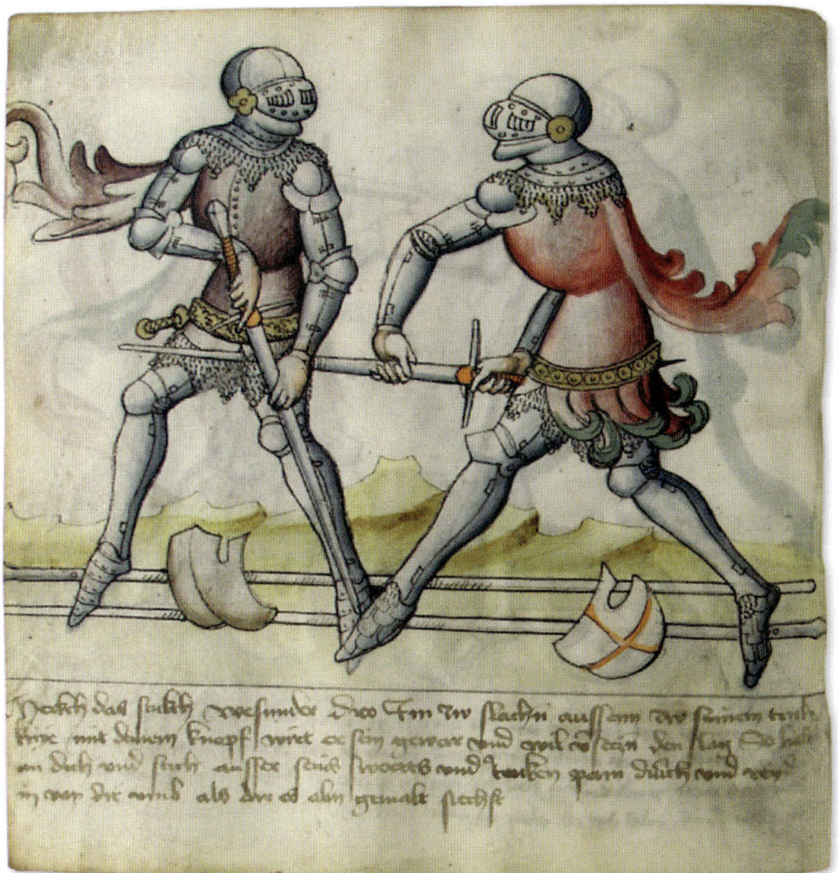

Merkch das stukch wesunder Dw Im zw slachen aussenn zw seinem tenkn knÿe mit deinem knopf wirt er sein gewar vnd vnd wil verseczen den slag So halt an dich vnd stich ausser seins swertts vnder tenken pain durch vnd reyd in von dir vmb als dw es oben gemalt siechst

27R (26R)

Note the work[16] of the plate gauntlet. If he throws himself around towards you, and attempts to twist himself out, then step in front of his left foot to the outside with your left foot. Grab him around his whole body with your left arm and hold your point strongly in his gauntlet. Thus you will throw him. However, if he has brought you into the same situation as you did to him before, turn to him and hit his left arm behind his elbow with your right hand to move him away from you. Thus you will free yourself from him.

16 See note 14.

xxiii *While* Gladiatoria *Vienna has the same text, the one in* Gladiatoria *Cracow is completely different.*

xxiv *Interestingly, this is one of only two images showing fighters with gauntlets. In the present manuscript, the chronological order is mixed up since the second action with gauntlets, which is on fol. 28v, is situated before this one in both* Gladiatoria *Cracow and Vienna; this is also in line with the actual sequence of the technique.*

[xxiii] *Merkch die arbaitt des plechhantschuech*[xxiv] *ob er sich gegenn dir vmb würff vnd sich aus reydenn wolt So schraitt mit deinem tenkn fues für seynn tenken fues ausserhalbn vnd greyff ym mit deinem tenkn arm vorn vmb seinen ganczn leib halt dein ortt vast in seinem hantschuech So wirffstu in ob er dich hett d[ar] zw pracht als ÿm vor wider varen ist So cher dich gen ÿm vnd stoos mit de[iner] rechten hant an seinen tenkn arm hinder den ellpogenn von dir so wirstu von Im [ledig]*

27V (26v) SWORD

Note the piece. If you both thrust at each other towards the face outside of your swords, then press his point strongly upwards with your sword. Step through with your left foot between his two feet. Grab around his body with your left arm, and his left knee-bend with your pommel. Thus you will throw him, as you see painted above.

xxv *Recte "vmb", s. a.* Gladiatoria *Cracow and Vienna.*

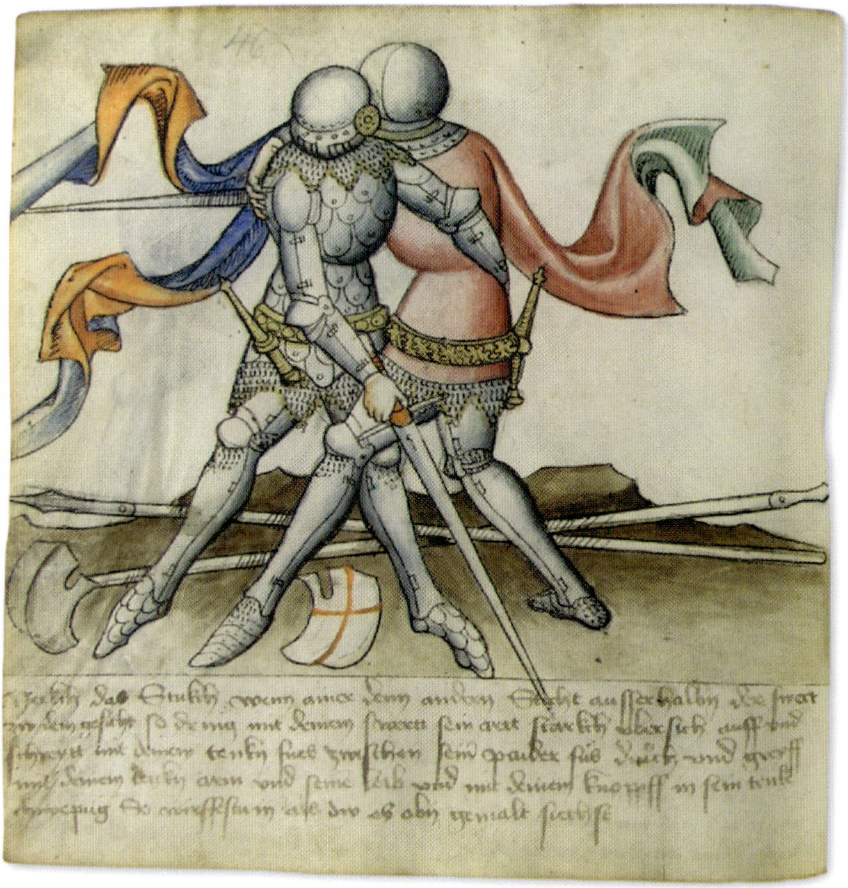

Merkch das Stukch wenn ainer denn andern Sticht ausserhalbn der swert zw dem gesicht so dring mit deinem swertt sein ortt starkch vbersich auff vnd schreytt mit deinem tenkn fues zwischen seiner paider füs durch vnd greyff mit deinem tenkn arm vnd[xxv] *seinem leib vnd mit deinem knoppff in sein tenke chnyepüg So wirffestu in als dw es obn gemalt siechst*

28R (25R)

Note the break. If he strives to throw you backwards in this manner, then grab him under his left armpit over his neck with your left arm. Step with your left foot to the outside of his left foot, and grasp around his left arm above the elbow with your right hand. Throw him down at your feet, as you see painted above.

Merkch den pruch wenn er dich hett welln also werffenn vber rukch So greyff in mit deinem tenkn arm vber seynn hals vnder sein rechtte vgsenn vnd schre[yt] mit deinem tenkn fües ausserhalb seins tenkn fues vnd greyff mit deiner rechtn hant vmb seinen tenkn arm ob des ellpogen vnd wirff in gegenn dir nyder als dw es obn gemalt siechst

28v (25v)

Note the piece. In this, the thrust comes towards the gauntlet and frees it from pressing on the breast. Once you have secured him with your point, shove him away from you, as you see painted above.

Merkch das stukch dauon kumbt der stich zw dem hantschuech vnd nymbt sich von den dringen zw der prust wenn dw in hast geheft mit deinem ortt So schewb in von dir als dw es obn gemalt siechst

29R (31R)

Note the piece. When both of you strive to grasp each other and wrestle, and he grasps you with his right hand, then hit his right arm over the elbow with your left hand. Step forward with your right foot to the outside of his right foot, and grasp around his body with your right arm. Thus you will throw him over your hip, as you see painted above.

Merkch das stukch als sÿ zw ein ander welln greyffen zw ringen ob [er] mit seiner rechten hant nach dir greyfft So stos mit deiner tenkchen hant an seinen rechten arm ob des ellpogen vnd schreyt mit deinem rechten fues für ausserhalb seins rechten fües vnd greyff mit deinem rechten arm vmb seinen leib So wirffestu In vber dein huff als dw es oben gemalt sichst

29V (31V)

Note the piece. If both of you have grasped each other's arms and are pulling strongly, then let your left hand go. Use the hand to hit his right arm behind the elbow to the inside to drive it away from yourself. Grasp around his back with your right arm, and with your left hand, grasp his right foot below the knee from the outside. Lift up, and thus you will throw him as you see painted above.

Merkch das stukch wenn zwen aInn den andern die arm vest begriffen hatt vnd vast rukn So la aus dein tenke hantt vnd stös damit seinen rechtn arm hindern ellpogen einwerts von dir vnd greyff mit deinem rechtn arm vber seinen rukch vnd mit deiner tenkn hant von aussenn an seinen rechten fües vnderm knÿe vnd heb vber sich So wirffestu In als dw es oben gemalt sichst

30R (32R) DAGGER

Note the beginning of six pieces with the dagger from which all wrestling techniques of the limbs, all pieces with the dagger, and the breaks that belong to them are derived. Note whether he has raised his dagger high towards the left side of his shoulder, with his [left] foot forwards.

xxvi *"anvankch" and "degn" have been underlined in pencil by a later hand.*

xxvii *Since this image appears only in* Gladiatoria *Vienna—unfortunately without text—but not in the version from Cracow, a completion cannot be provided here. The illustration, however, suggests the left foot.*

Merkch den anvankch[xxvi] Sechs stukch des degn[xxvii] daraus alle ringen kom[en] der gelidmas daraus kömen alle Stukch die der degen Inne hat vnd sei[n] wider pruch die dar auff gehorn Merkch ob er seinen degen hett auff g[e] czukcht In dÿ hoch auff zw der tenkchen seytten seiner agsl zw vnd sein [?][xxvii] füs hett für geseczett

30V (32V) DAGGER

Note the second piece.[17] When he thrusts towards your face with his dagger from above, catch his right hand by the wrist in your left hand. Twist his arm outwards, and thus you have broken his thrust. If you wish to wrestle with him, let go of your dagger and grasp his right elbow from below with your right hand. Pull inwards to your chest, and thus you will break his arm or he must fall.

17 In the versions from both Cracow and Vienna, this is the first dagger technique.

Merkch das ander stukch ob er dir stech von oben zw dem gesichtt mit seinem degn So vach sein rechte hantt bey dem glid in dein tenke hant vnd reyd ym seÿnn arm auswerts So hastu Im den stich geprochen wildw in bringen zw ringen so lass deinen degenn vnd greyff mit deiner rechten hant von vnden auff sein rechten ellpogn vnd rukch einttwerts gen der brust So prichstu Im den arm oder er mües vallenn

31R (33R)

Note one more dagger piece.[18] If he thrusts towards your breast from above and was so quick that you could not reach your dagger, then grasp his hand behind his dagger with your right hand. Strike your left arm over his right arm and set your left hand on your breast. Draw your right hand strongly towards yourself, and thus you will break his arm or throw him down at your feet as you see painted above.

18 This dagger technique is not numbered in the text. Consecutive numbering begins again only with the next, the third piece.

Merkch mer ain stukch des degenn ob er dir von obn zw der prust stech vnd vber eylt hiett das dw zw deinem degenn nicht hettest mügen komen So vach m[it] deiner rechtn hantt sein hentt hinder seÿnn degenn vnd slach deinen tenkchen arm oben vber seinen rechten arm vnd secz dein tenke hant an dein prust vnd drukch dein rechtte hantt vast zu dir So prichestu seÿnn arm oder wirffe[st] In für dein nÿder als dw es obn gemalt sichst

31V (33V)

Note the third dagger piece. If he thrusts towards your body from below and you could not take hold of your dagger, grasp his wrist behind his dagger from above with your right hand and grasp his elbow from below with your left hand. Lift his arm to your left shoulder, and thus you will break his arm or carry him wherever you wish, as you see painted above.

Merkch das dritt stukch des degenn ob er von vnttn stëch zu dem ganczn leib vnd dw zw deinem degenn nicht kömen wärest So greyff von obn mit deiner rechten hantt auff sein glid hindter seins degenn vnd mit deiner tenkn hantt von vntten an seinen ellpogen vnd heb seinen arm auff auff dein tenken achsell So zeprichestu seynn arm oder tregst In wo dw In wilt als dw es oben gemalt sichst

32R (34R)

Note the fourth piece. If he thrusts at your face from above, then let go of your dagger, and grasp his hand behind his dagger with your left hand. Grasp his blade with your turned right hand, and thus you will take his dagger and lead him wherever you wish, as you see painted above.

Merkch das vyerd stukch ob er dir von oben stech zw dem gesicht So lass deinenn degn vnd vach in dein tenke hantt sein hant hinden degenn vnd greiff mit deiner vercherten rechten hant in sein chlingn So nymbstu ym seynn degenn vnd pringst in zw wew dw wild als dw es oben gemalt sichst

32V (34V)

Note the fifth piece. If he thrusts upwards from his right side to your body, then grasp his arm behind the dagger with your left hand, and [grasp] the blade with your right hand. Twist downwards, and thus you will take his dagger, as you see painted above.

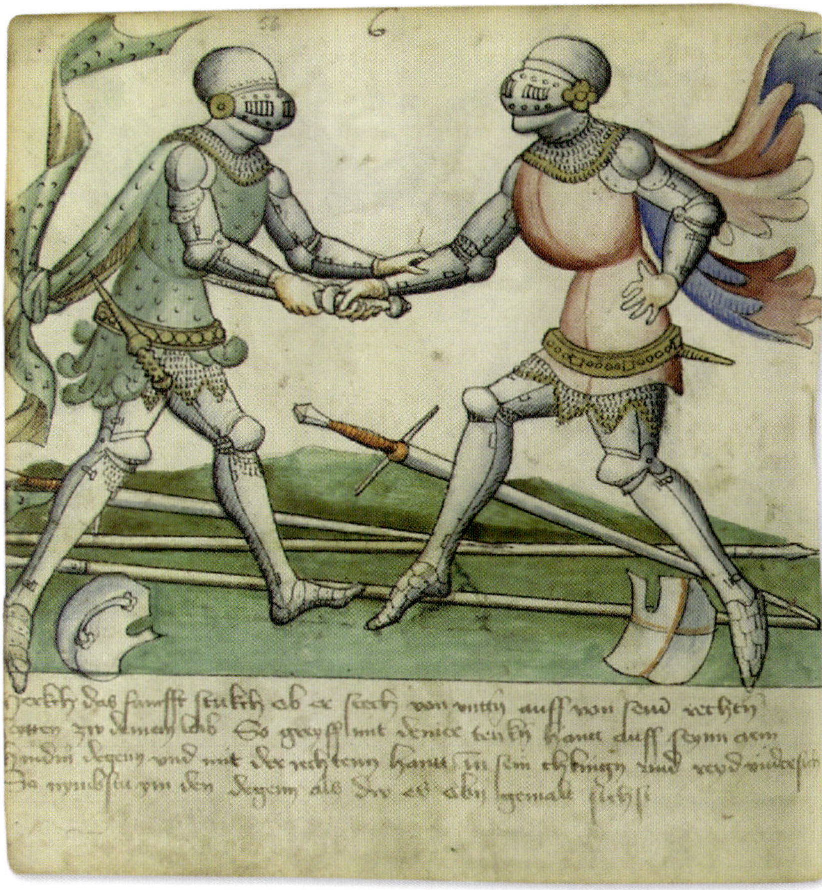

Merkch das funfft stukch ob er stech von vntten auff von seiner rechten seytten zw deinem leib So greyff mit deiner tenken hantt auff seynn arm hinderm degenn vnd mit der rechtenn hantt In sein chlingn vnd reyd ündersich So nymbstu ym den degenn als dw es obn gemalt sichst

33R (35R)

Note the sixth piece. If he thrusts at your neck from his left shoulder, then catch his hand behind the dagger with your left hand. Grasp his blade with your right hand and lift upwards. Thus you will take his dagger. Step to the outside with your left foot, behind his right foot, and strike his breast with your right hand. Thus you will bring him over your leg to fall. You may see the beginning of this painted above.

Merkch das Sechst stukch ob er stech von seiner tenkn agsl zw deinem hals
So vach mitt deiner tenken hantt sein hant hindern degenn vnd greiff mitt
deiner rechten hantt in sein klingen vnd heb vbersich so nymbstu Im seynn
degenn vnd schreitt mit deinem tenkn fues aussenn hinder seinen rechtn
fües vnd stos mit deiner rechten hantt in sein brust So vellestu In vber
dein pain als dw des anefang obn gemalt sichst

33V (35V)

Note the seventh piece, one of the five parries.[19] If he thrusts at your face from above, then catch the thrust on your dagger between your hands. When you have parried the thrust, then quickly grasp his right elbow from below with your left hand. With your right foot, step behind his left foot to the outside, and lift his arm up strongly. Thus you will throw him backwards, as you see painted above.

19 A defending and blocking action.

Merkch das Sybent stukch der funff versaczung aine ob er dir von oben stech zw dem gesichtt So vach den stich zwischen dein hentt auff deynn degenn wenn dw ym den stich hast versecztt So greyff resch mit deiner tenken hantt von vntten auff seinen rechten ellpogen vnd schreit mit deinem rechtn füs aussn hinder seynen tenken fues vnd heb seinen arm vast vbersich So wirfesstu in vber rukch als dw es obn gemalt siechst

34R (36R)

Note the eighth piece. If he thrusts towards your body from below with strength, then drop your dagger, which you hold between your two hands, onto his blade. Thus you will parry his thrust. With your left hand, grasp his wrist behind the dagger, and step to the outside in front of his right foot with your right foot. Grasp his neck on the left side with your right hand, and thus you can throw him down well. You may see the beginning of this painted above.

Merkch das achtt stukch ob er dir stech mit krafft von vndn zw deinez leib So vall mit deinem degen zwischn bayder deiner hentt auff sein chlingen So hastw ўm den stich versecztt vnd greyff mit deiner tenkn hant auff sein glid hindern degen vnd schreitt mit deinem rechtn fues nach aussn für seinen rechtn fues vnd greyff mit deiner rechten hantt an dўe tenkch seytten seins hals So magstu in wol werffenn dernyder als dw den anfankch oben gemalt sichst

Note the ninth piece. If he puts his right foot in front, and thrusts towards your breast from his left side, then catch the thrust on the blade between your two hands. With your left hand, grasp his arm behind the elbow, and push strongly away from yourself, so that he turns his back towards you. You may see the beginning of this painted above.

Merkch das Newnt stukch ob er seinen rechten fues hett fur geseczt vnd stech von sein tenkn seyttn zw deiner prust So vach den stich czwischenn bäyd deiner hentt auff dein chlingn vnd greyff nach mit deiner tenkn hant auff seynn arm hindern ellpogenn vnd stoos vast von dir das er dir den rukch kertt als dw es oben den anfankch gemalt sichst

35R (37R)

Note the tenth piece. If he thrusts at your face from above, and you were unable to get hold of your dagger, then lay your right hand on the left crosswise, and catch the thrust on your arms. With your left hand, grasp around his wrist behind the dagger, and with your right hand, [grasp] his blade upwards from below. Thus you will take his dagger. You may see the beginning of this painted above.

Merkch das zehentt stukch ob er von oben zw dem gesicht stech vnd zw deinem
degen nicht komen werest So leg dein rechte hant auff die tenkche krewczweys
vnd vach den stich auff deinen arm vnd greyff mit deiner tenken hant vmb
sein glid hinderwerts degen vnd mit der rechten hant vbersich auff In sein ch[lingen]
So nymbstu ymb seÿnn degenn als dw den anevang obn gemalt sichst

35V (37V)

Note the eleventh piece. If he thrusts at your breast from below from the right side, and puts his left foot strongly forwards, and you have failed to reach for your dagger, then drop your crossed hands on his dagger from above. With your left hand, grasp his hand behind the dagger from above, and grasp his blade with your right. Press down, and thus you will take his dagger. You may see the beginnings of this painted above.

Merkch das Aindlefft Stukch ob er von vndtn aus der rechten seÿten stech zu dein prust vnd seinen tenken fües hatt fürgesacztt nach stakch vnd dw deins degenn [ver]sawmt wärest So vall aber mit deinen hentten krewczweis von obn auff seinen [d]egn vnd greyff mit deiner tenkn hantt oben auff sein hant hindeen degenn [v]nd greyff mit deiner rechten hant in sein kchlingn vnd drukch vndersich So nymbstu im seÿnn degenn als dw den anfanch obn gemalt sichst

36R (39R)

Note the fourteenth piece. If he thrusts downwards at you from above with all of his strength, then parry against his thrust from your right side. Afterwards, hit his right elbow with your left hand so that he turns his back to you. Drive the dagger through his two legs from behind, pull him to you, and grasp the back of his neck with your left hand. Thus you will throw him down in front of yourself, as you see painted above.

xxviii Pieces 12 and 13 are missing.

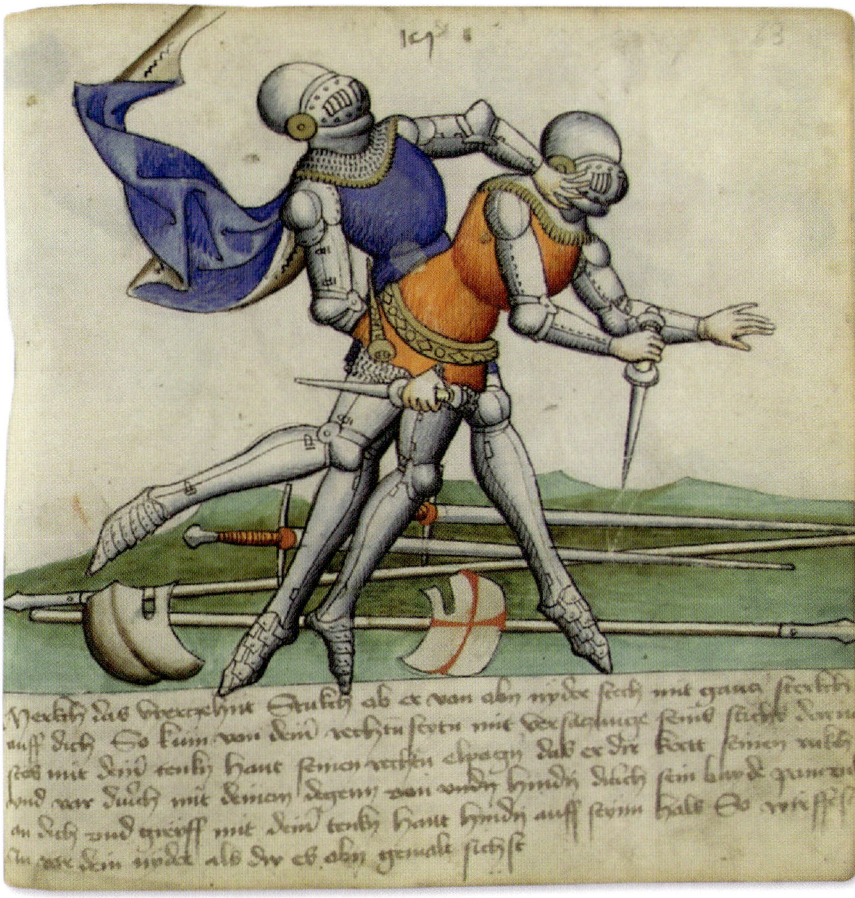

Merkch das vyerczehnt[xxviii] Stukch ob er von obn nÿder stech mit ganczer sterkch auff dich So küm von deiner rechten seytn mit versaczunge seins stichs dar na[ch] stös mit deiner tenkn hant seinen rechten elpogen das er dir kertt seinen rukch vnd var durch mit deinem degenn von ~~vndn~~ hinden durch sein bayde pain ruk[ch] an dich vnd greÿff mit deiner tenkn hant hindn auff seÿnn hals So wirffestu In vor dein nÿder als dw es obn gemalt sichst

36v (39v) DAGGER

Note the fifteenth piece. If both thrust at each other towards the face from the upper right side, and both come close to one another with the parry, then hit his right arm from below with your left arm. Grasp his neck with your left hand, and grasp his legs by going between them with your dagger. Pull towards you, thus you will throw him, as you see painted above.

xxix *Recte "pain", see* Gladiatoria *Cracow and Vienna.*

Merkch das funfczehnt stukch ob ainer den andern stech von obn von der rechten seytten zw dem gesichtt vnd bayd mit versaczung an einander kämen warn So stos mit deinem tenken arm von vntten auff seinen rechten arm vnd greyff mit deiner tenken hant an seynn hals vnd greyff mit deinem degen zwischen sein pant[xxix] *durch rukch an dich So wirffestu In als dw es obn gemalt sichst*

37R (40R) DAGGER

Note the sixteenth piece. If he thrusts downwards at you from above towards your neck, and you were not able to reach for your dagger, then catch his arm with both hands. Twist his dagger inwards and his elbow outwards, and put your left foot in front of his left foot to the outside.[20] Thus you will throw him as you see painted above.

20 In fact, the illustration shows the left foot on the *inside,* which makes the throw much more difficult to perform. *Gladiatoria* Cracow is mostly identical. However, the position of the feet in the Vienna version is not so clear, and the foot could indeed be placed on the outside.

Merkch das Sechczehnt stukch ob er dir von obn nyder stech zw dem hals vnd dw zw deinem degen nicht komen werst So vach seinen arm in bayd deine hendt vnd reyd einttwerts seynn degen vnd den ellpogen auswerts vnd secz deinen tenkn fues aussenn für seynn tenken fues So wirffestu In als dw es oben gemalt sichst etc

37V (40v) DAGGER

Note the seventeenth piece. When he thrusts at you from above, then grasp around his wrist behind his dagger with your turned left hand, so that his blade comes to the outside of your arm. Step to the outside of his right foot with your right foot, and hit his neck with your right hand. Thus you will throw him, as you see painted above.

Merkch das Sybenczehnt Stukch ob er von obn stech auff dich So greyff mit deiner verkertten tenken hantt hinder seinen degen vmb sein glid vnd das sein kling aussenn auff den arm kem vnd schreytt mit deinem rechtn fues ausserhalb seins rechten fues vnd stos mit deiner rechten hant an seinen hals So wirffestu In Als dw es oben gemalt sichst

38R (47R)

Note the thirtieth piece, which is the break to the wrestling from the change.[21] If he grabbed your left thigh, and put his left arm on the right side of your neck, then strike his wrist behind the dagger with your left hand, and twist his arm around, so that he turns his back towards you. This way you have broken his wrestling from the change, as you see painted before and above.

21 A technique described in the preceding piece, which is missing here.

xxx *Pieces 18 to 29 are missing.*

Merkch das dreyssigist[xxx] Stukch das ist der pruch auff das Ringen des wechsll ob er dir nach deinem tenken diech hett gegriffenn vnd hett geseczt seinen tenkn arm an die rechtt seytten deines hals So stös mit deiner tenkn hant auff sein glid hindern degenn vnd reid seinen arm vmb daz er dir kertt seynn rukg So hastu Im das ringen aus dem wechsell geprochn als dw es vor vnd oben gemalt sichst etc

Note the thirty-first piece. If both have grasped each other in the same way, and each has brought his right arm under the left armpit of the other, and one has strongly swung the other one, and you have then brought him to your left side for the throw, then step forwards to the outside of his right leg. Swing strongly onwards with your right arm, and thus you will throw him downwards, as you see painted above.

Merkch das Ainvnddreyssigist Stukch ob sy bed geleich ainer den andren hett gevassett vnd yeder seinen rechten arm vnder sein tenke vgsenn pracht vnd ainer den andren herttikchleich Swung wenn dw in hast pracht in den Swung deiner tenken seyttenn So tritt für aussenhalb seins rechten pain aussen für sein rechts pain vnd swing mit deinem rechten arm vast nach So wirffestu In nyder auf den rukch als dw es obn gemalt sichst

39R (49R)

Note the thirty-fourth piece of wrestling, which comes from the break of the change. When he puts his right arm on your neck, and strives to grab your leg above your knee with his left hand to throw you backwards, then catch his hand behind his dagger with your right hand and strike it into his groin. Step with your right foot so that you come behind his back. With your left hand, grab through his two legs from behind, and grasp his wrist behind the dagger. Then let your right hand go, and grasp him over the breast with it from the outside. Thus you will throw him, as you see painted above.

xxxi *Pieces 32 and 33 are missing.*

xxxii *"rechten" (= right) according to* Gladiatoria *Cracow and Vienna, which is also much more in line with the flow of the piece.*

Merkch das vyervnddreÿssigist[xxxi] *Stukch des ringen kumbt er aus dem pruch der wechsl ob er dir hett geseczlt sein rechtn arm an deinen hals vnd hett welln greyffenn mit seiner tenkn hant nach deinem pain ob deins knyes vnd wolt dich werffenn vber rukch So vach mit deiner tenkn*[xxxii] *hant sein hant hindern degen vnd slach Ims in sein schos vnd schreyt mit deinem rechtn fues das dw Im kümbst hinder seinen rukch greyff mit deiner tenkn hant von hindn durch pede seine pain in sein glid hindern degen So la varn dein rechte hant vnd greyf damit von ausse[n vber sein] prust So wirffestu In als dw es oben gemalt sichst*

39V (49V)

Note the thirty-fifth piece. If he has put his left foot forward, and thrusts towards your face from his right shoulder from above, then catch his right arm behind the elbow with your right hand. Strike his left shoulder, and grasp above his right arm with your left. Push strongly downwards, and thus you will break his arm or throw him down, as you see painted above.

Merkch das funnff vnddreyssigist Stukch ob er hett seinen tenkn fües für geseczt vnd stech von obn nyder zw deinem gesicht von seiner rechtn agsell So vach mit deiner rechtn hant seinen rechten arm hinderm der ellpogn vnd slach ym auff sein tenks agsell vnd greyff mit deinem tenken arm obn vber seinen rechtn vnd druckch vast nÿder So brichst ym den arm oder wirfst nyder als dws obn gemalet sichst

40R (50R)

Note the thirty-sixth [piece]. If he puts his right foot forward, and thrusts downwards at you with all of his strength from above, and strives to rush in at you, so that you can't reach for your weapons, then throw your left arm over his right arm and pull so that you bring it under your left armpit. Step in front of his left foot to the outside with your left foot, and pull towards yourself. Thus you will throw him, as you see painted above.

xxxiii Gladiatoria *Cracow does not contain this piece at all, and the Vienna version presents the illustration, but not the text. Completions following other manuscripts must therefore be omitted.*

Merkch das Sechs vnddreyssigst ob er seinen rēchkn fues hett für geseczt vnd s[tech?][xxxiii]
von seiner ganczn krafft von oben nyder auff dich vnd dich wolt vber eylln das dw
zw deiner wer nicht wërst kömen So slach von obn nÿder mit deinem tenkn
armm uber seinen rechtn arm vnd rukchen das dw In pringst vnder deine tenk[?]
ügsen vnd schreit mit deinem tenken fües aussn fur seinen tenkn fus vnd ru[kch]
gegen dir So wirffestu In aks dws obn gemalt sichst

Note the [piece]. If he thrusts upwards at you from below from his right side, and he has put his left foot forwards, then step inside his feet with your left foot and drop your left hand onto his right hand. Grab his blade with your right hand, and twist the point upwards towards his breast. Thus you will push his dagger into him, as you see painted above.

This is the thirty-seventh piece with the dagger.

xxxiv *The word "stuck" is missing here (see* Gladiatoria *Vienna).*

xxxv *"den" (= the), instead of "dein" (= your), according to* Gladiatoria *Cracow and Vienna, which would be more in line with the flow of the piece anyway.*

Merkch das[xxxiv] ob er von vndn auff stech von seine rechten seytten vnd seinen tenkn fües hett für sacztt So schreytt mit deinem tenkn fües Innerhalb seins fües vnd vall mit deiner tenkn hant auff sein rechte hant vnd greyff mit deiner rechtn hant auff sein chling vnd reÿd vbersich auff dein[xxxv] ort In sein prust So drukchst dw seinen degen in In als dw es obn gemalt sichst

Das ist das xxxvij stukch des degens

41R (52R) HOLDING DOWN

Note the third holding piece. When you have begun to wrestle with him, and you grasp him with your left arm in front around his neck, then drop downwards on your left knee, pull him downwards towards yourself on his back, and work[22] with your dagger, as you see painted above.

22 That is, attacking, seeking and exploiting the openings. See note 14.

xxxvi Pieces one and two are missing.

Merkch das dritt[xxxvi] *Stukch des halten wenn du mit Im zw ringn bist komen vnd hast Im griffen mit deinem tenkn arm voren vmb seinen hals So vall nÿder auff dein tenkchs knÿe vnd rukch In zw dir dar nyder auf seinen rukn vnd aribait mit deinem degen als dw es l [!] oben gemalt siechst*

41V (52V) HOLDING DOWN

Note the fourth holding piece. If you have again brought him to his back with wrestling, then drop with your right knee between his legs, and push his right arm down near the shoulder with your left elbow. Lift his visor up at the bevor[23] with the same hand, and work with your dagger, as you see painted above.

23 A *bevor* is usually a stand-alone piece of armour that was worn in combination with the type of helmet known as a sallet. It was a chin protection, attached to the armour by the means of staples, pins, and leather straps. Quite often, the sallet was worn entirely without a bevor. Calling the chin protection of a closed visored helmet a bevor is rather unusual.

xxxvii Recte: "drukch", as in Gladiatoria *Cracow and Vienna.*

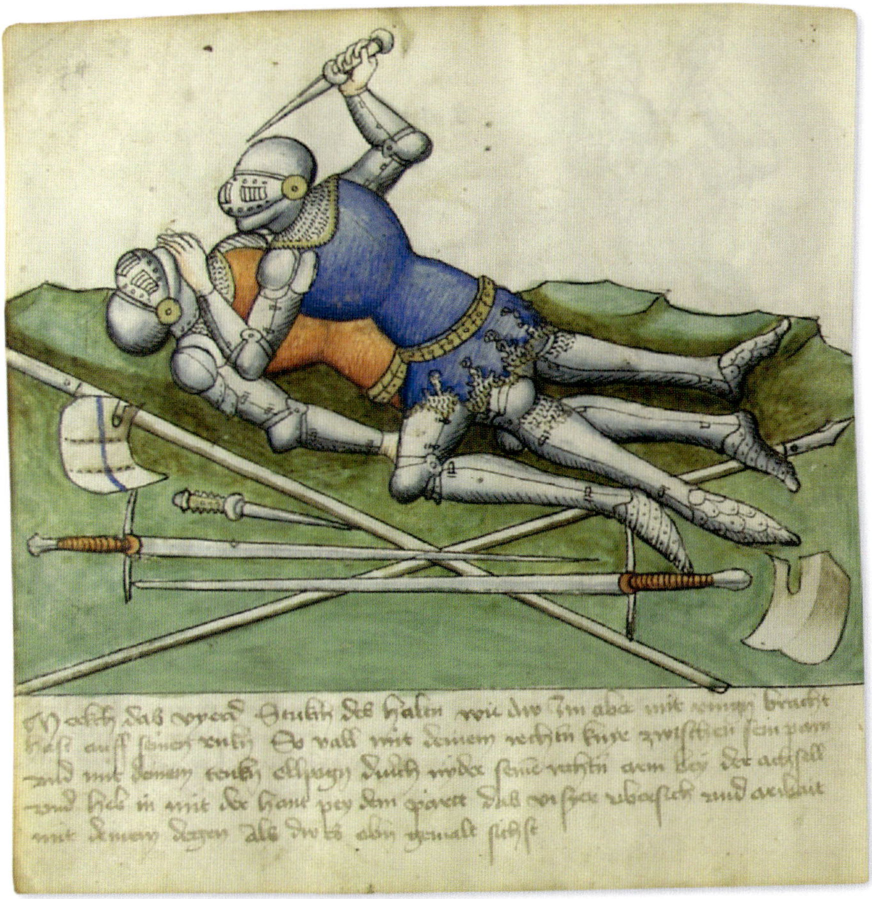

Merkch das vyerd Stukch des halten wie dw Im aber mit ringen bracht
hast auff seinen rukn So vall mit deinem rechten knye zwischen sein pain
vnd mit deinem tenkn ellpogn durch[xxxvii] *nýder seinen rechten arm bey der achsell*
vnd heb in mit der hant pey dem partt das visyer vbersich vnd aribait
mit deinem degen Als dw es oben gemalt sichst

42R (53R) HOLDING DOWN

Note the fifth holding piece. If it so happens that you have again thrown him on his back, then drop downwards on your left knee to the outside of his left leg. If he pulls his foot towards himself, and strives to support himself in standing up, then go under his left knee-bend from the outside with your left hand. Grab his right hand by the wrist, hold it tight and work with your dagger, as you see painted above.

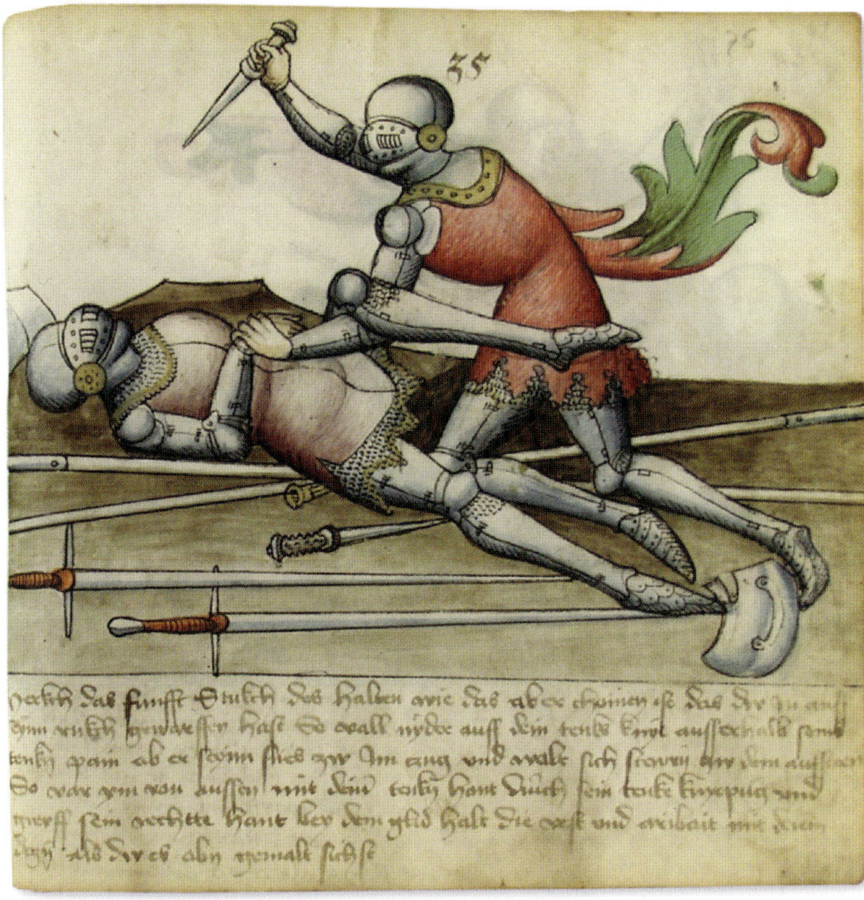

Merkch das funfft Stukch des halten wie das aber chömen ist das dw In auff seynn rukch geworffen hast So vall nÿder auff dein tenks knÿe ausserhalb seins tenkn pain ob er seÿnn fües zw Im czug vnd wolt sich stewren zw dem aufsteen So var ym von aussen mit deiner tenken hant durch sein tenke knyepug vnd greyff sein rechtte hant bey dem glid halt die vest vnd aribait mit deinem degen als dw es obn gemalt sichst

42V (53V) HOLDING DOWN

Note the sixth holding piece. If it so happens that you have thrown him on his belly during wrestling, then drop downwards with your right knee next to his right leg, and your left knee on his loin. If he lifts himself on both his arms, and thus strives to stand up, then hit his right arm under his breast with your right hand, grasp his left hand by the wrist with your left hand, turn it behind his back, and hold tight. Draw your dagger, and work, as you see painted above.

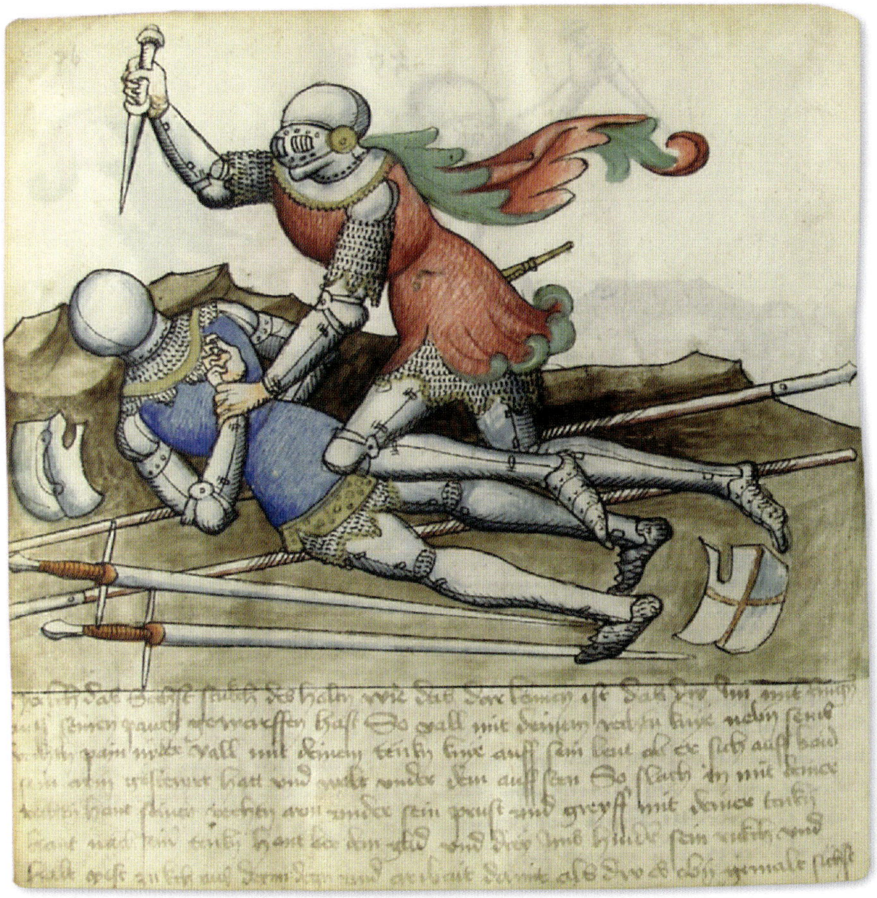

Merkch das Sechst stukch des haltn wie das dar kömen ist das dw Im mit Ringen auff seinen pauch geworffen hast So vall mit deinem rechten knÿe neben seins rechtn pain nÿder vall mit deinem tenkn knÿe auff sein lent ob er sich auff baid sein arm gestewrt hatt vnd wolt vnder dem auff sten So slach in mit deiner rechtn hant seinen rechtn arm vnder sein prust vnd greyff mit deiner tenken hant nach seiner tenkn hant bey dem glid vnd dreÿ Ims hinder sein rukch vnd halt vest zukch aus deinn degn vnd aribait damit als dw es oben gemalt sichst

43R (54R) HOLDING DOWN

Note the seventh holding piece. If it so happens that you brought him to his back during wrestling, then fall with your right knee between his both legs. Take his left hand into your left hand, and pull it under his head. Hold it tight, and work at his face, as you see painted above.

xxxviii *The Cracow version offers some more detail here:*
"vnd greÿff mit deinem rechten fueß über seinen tencken rist so helst du In den fueß daz er daz pain nicht mag an sich gezihen".
(Go with your right foot over his left instep. Thus you secure his foot so that he cannot pull the leg towards himself.)

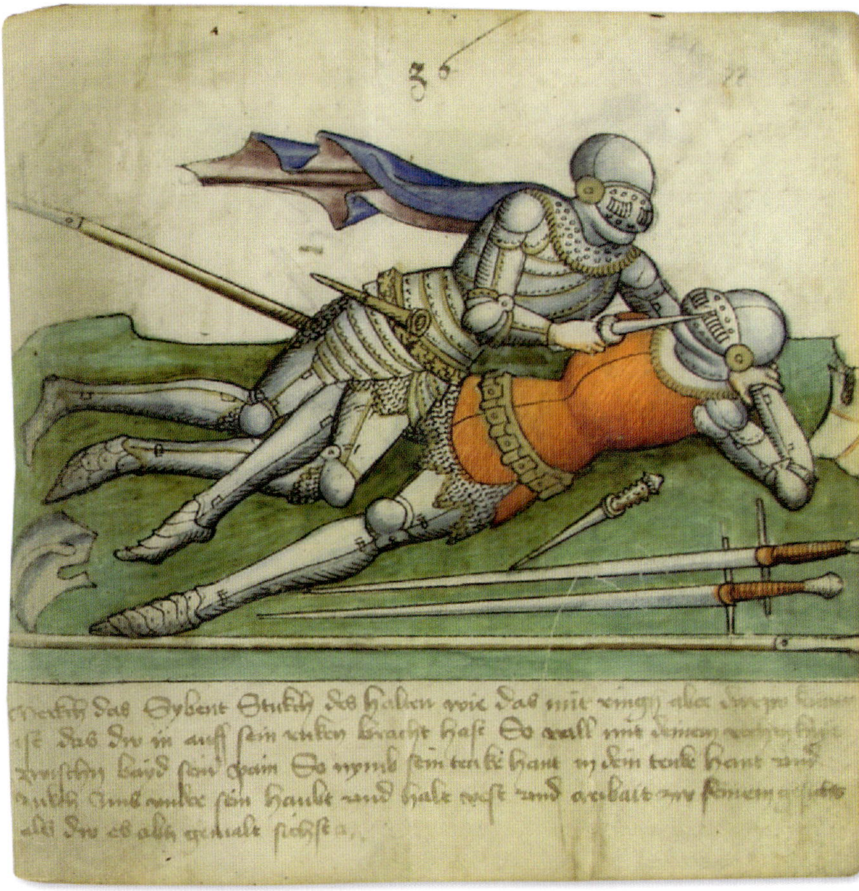

Merkch das Sybent Stukch des halten wie das mit ringen aber darzw kümen ist das dw in auff sein ruken bracht hast So vall mit deinem rechtn knÿe zwischn bayd seiner pain[xxxviii] *So nymb sein tenke hant in dein tenke hant vnd zukch Ims vnder sein haubt vnd halt vest vnd aribait zw seinem gesicht als dw es obn gemalt sichst*

43V (54V)

DIERK HAGEDORN

A LONG TIME AGO ...

DIERK HAGEDORN

A LONG TIME AGO IN A LIBRARY FAR, FAR AWAY …

The Adventures of the *Gladiatoria* Manuscript from New Haven

I. THE DESCRIPTION

How nice it is when something you believed to be irretrievably lost finally reappears: the missing little red toy car, the untraceable wedding ring, the runaway pet—or the medieval fencing manuscript.

Quite frequently, these missing items are not really lost at all, but only misplaced somewhere else. And this is exactly what happened to the manuscript we will discuss here.

Codex MS U860.F46 1450 from the Yale Center for British Art (YCBA) in New Haven, Connecticut, has had a rather exciting and trying time, upon which we will now attempt to shed some light. It is a Fechtbuch—a book that deals with fighting techniques—that was originally only one part of a larger entity, *Codex Gothanus Membr. II 109* from the Herzogliche Bibliothek in Gotha in Germany, which disappeared from the library during or shortly after World War II. We will only deal extensively with this first part, the one containing the Fechtbuch, and will begin by describing it. The fate of the original, entire manuscript will be briefly outlined later on.

Everything concerning our manuscript is ambiguous, even difficult. As such, we will encounter uncertainties and oddities time and again over the course of this brief essay. Even the format exemplifies this characteristic.

Format

In the original shelf mark from Gotha—*Membr. II 109*—the Roman numeral "II" signifies a quarto book format.

The manuscript was measured at least five times in the past, each time with certain differences:

- In the first known description of the manuscript, Friedrich Jacobs and Friedrich August Ukert[1] came to a result of 6 × 6¼ French inches, which corresponds to 163 × 169 mm (or 6.42 × 6.65 in)—according to the conversion carried out by Hans-Peter Hils,[2]
- Walter Benary[3] measures 163 × 175 mm (6.42 × 6.89 in) in 1912,
- Cornelia Hopf[4] stated 16.5 × 17.5 cm (6.50 × 6.89 in) in 1997,
- the catalogue of the German illustrated manuscripts from the Middle Ages[5] from 2009 mentioned a size of 165 × 180 mm (6.50 × 7.09 in),
- and finally, the YCBA stated a format of about 19 x 20 cm (7.48 × 7.87 in) in 2012.

After a request from the author in August 2012, Francis Lapka, catalogue librarian of the YCBA, checked the measurements and determined a size of 172 x 185 mm (6.77 × 7.28 in) for the cover; the pages of the body of the book are consistently 165 × 178 mm (6.50 × 7.01 in)—apart from three leaves with their text cut off. These dimensions vary by less than one millimetre in total.[6]

The current format, however, is by no means the original one, since passages of the text have frequently been cropped at the outer and lower margins. The *Gladiatoria* manuscript from Vienna[7] is extraordinarily similar to this one in several aspects,

1 Jacobs/Ukert: *Beiträge zur ältern Litteratur oder Merkwürdigkeiten der Herzogl. öffentlichen Bibliothek zu Gotha*, p. 141.

2 Hils: "'Gladiatoria'. Über drei Fechthandschriften aus der ersten Hälfte des 15. Jahrhunderts'. – *Codices manuscripti,* Heft 1/2, 1987, p. 11.

3 Benary: "Ein unbekanntes handschriftliches Fragment einer Lope'schen Komödie". *Zeitschrift für Romanische Philologie 36* (1912) pp. 657–678; here: p. 658.

4 Hopf: *Die abendländischen Handschriften der Forschungs- und Landesbibliothek Gotha. Bestandsverzeichnis. 2. Kleinformatige Pergamenthandschriften Memb. II. Gotha: Forschungs- und Landesbibliothek*, p. 66f.

5 Frühmorgen-Voss/Ott/Bodemann/Stöllinger-Löser/Leng: *Katalog der deutschsprachigen illustrierten Handschriften des Mittelalters*, p. 23 ff.

6 Email correspondence from August 21, 2013.

7 *KK 5013*. Vienna: Kunsthistorisches Museum.

including in size and proportions. A direct comparison with the illustrations and texts of the Vienna manuscript—its size is listed as 185 x 195 mm (7.28 x 7.68 in)[8]—suggests that the New Haven manuscript was originally about one centimetre (or a little less than half an inch) higher and wider. It cannot be ascertained for sure when it was cropped, but Jacobs and Ukert had already mentioned damages.[9]

Cover

The cover consists of auburn leather. Five punched diagonals intersect each other on both the front and the back cover, thus forming rhombic fields. Two rows of three fields one above the other are shaped thus, and in each field, a narrow rhombus that is bordered by an outline carries a raised griffin rampant on a punched ground. Six more fields bear embossed flower heads in a circle: two smaller ones on top of another occupy the left and right side respectively, with two larger ones in the middle.

The spine is divided by four double raised bands. Between the second and the third, we find the golden embossed inscription "ARS PALAESTRA" (art of wrestling), beneath the fourth "XV s." (= the 15th century).

On the inside of the front cover, there is an oval ruby-coloured sticker with a central gold wheatsheaf and the words "Oak Spring" and "Paul Mellon" in golden letters running around it.

An insert has been glued to the inside of the back cover. It bears the YCBA logo and has the accession number written in pencil below: U860.F46 1450. The lower margin of the inside of the cover carries the embossed name of the bookbinder: S. (= Sven) Wiklander.

8 Frühmorgen-Voss/Ott/Bodemann/Stöllinger-Löser/Leng: *Katalog*, p. 30.
9 Jacobs/Ukert: *Beiträge*, p. 141.

Content

According to the information provided by the YCBA, the binding of the codex is neat. The manuscript begins with five empty leaves made of heavy paper resembling parchment; at the back, there is another such leaf. These leaves were inserted during the most recent binding in the 1960s.

The actual codex consists of 43 parchment leaves. The fashion of the binding is difficult to recognize without manhandling the manuscript too roughly. It appears, however, that some leaves are mounted on stubs, others by contrast are not. Unfortunately, the YCBA was unable to determine unequivocally whether the entire manuscript was bound together from single leaves. According to Francis Lapka "others appear to have conjugate leaves".[10]

All leaves are generally in a good condition, save for leaf number 7, which is much grubbier than the rest, and quite dilapidated.

Folios 1r–43r feature water coloured pen drawings in black ink over pencil sketches with two fighting persons in harness on each page. The pictures occupy the entire width and approximately the upper three-quarters of the page.

A pencil sketch is particularly identifiable at the right leg of the right fencer on f. 17v. This sketch corresponds to the stance found in the *Gladiatoria* manuscript from Vienna, f. 22v; the finished drawing, however, matches the version from Cracow,[11] f. 24v.

Beneath a separating line, three to eight lines of explanatory text are written in a blackletter script, called *bastarda*, with brown ink. Occasionally the text runs around the fighters' feet which overlap the separating line. This suggests that the drawings were outlined first with the text being filled in later in a next step. On some leaves, however, the text has been cut off beneath the fighting pairs, specifically on ff. 3, 4, and 7.

Only one scribe was involved in the execution of the manuscript, and he was also responsible for the majority of the Vienna *Gladiatoria* manuscript, revealed by close comparison of the two examples of handwriting (ff. 1r–10v,[12] 12r–27v, and 29r–56v). Occasionally, even the alignment of the single lines is identical in both manuscripts.

10 Email correspondence from August 21, 2013.

11 *Ms. Germ. Quart. 16*. Cracow: Biblioteka Jagiellońska.

12 In the *Katalog der deutschsprachigen illustrierten Handschriften des Mittelalters* erroneously indicated as 11v.

The dialect is Austro-Bavarian.[13]

Folio 43v features several Spanish names, written in pencil, possibly in the 17th century: Don Diego de Coes (twice), Juan Perez del Gurca, Jusepe Cerdeño.[14]
Almost all pages carry at least one numbering. However, these are inconsistent and incomplete:

- Fencing techniques, numbered consecutively in the text
  - in spear fighting (ff. 1r–5r, whereby the text is missing on leaves 3 and 4)
  - in dagger fighting (ff. 30r–40r)
  - in holding down techniques[15] (ff. 41r–43v)
- Possibly contemporary leaf numbering in ink
  - leaves 9–18
  - leaves 28–32
  - leaves 39–43
- Possibly contemporary leaf number in ink (ff. 25r and 37r)
- Possibly contemporary page numbering in ink (ff. 30r–37v)
- Page numbering in ink, probably from a later era (ff. 1r–6v)
- Page or leaf number in ink from a later (?) era (f. 7r)
- Modern in pencil (all pages except leaves 11, 18, 22, and 26)
- Modern pencil number 2, in a circle, on f. 22r

Since the current order of leaves got a bit mixed up—particularly in the middle part—these numberings may help us to reconstruct the initial configuration. More on this a little later.

Every page of the *Fechtbuch* shows two fighters in full armour[16] who fight against each other in a variety of disciplines:

1r–5r: Spear

5v–19v: Sword

13 Corresponding to the information for the codex from Vienna in the *Katalog der deutschsprachigen illustrierten Handschriften des Mittelalters*, p. 30.

14 Benary, loc. cit., p. 659.

15 This term signifies fighting techniques on the ground. Once the opponent was brought down he was to be immobilised and forced to surrender, often using a dagger. See also Martin Huntfelt's holding down techniques in *codex 44 A 8*, Rome: Biblioteca dell'Accademia Nazionale dei Lincei e Corsiniana, ff. 90v–93r.

16 See also "Offence and Defence", p. 17.

20r–22r: Wrestling
22v–28v: Sword
29r–29v: Wrestling
30r–40v: Dagger
41r–43r: Holding down

Wrestling, however, is not listed as an independent discipline, especially when we use the Cracow codex as a reference for comparison. In that volume, we find 50 consecutively numbered techniques for the sword between spear and dagger combat, and the wrestling techniques are included in these.

The suits of armour are depicted in minute detail, with coloured doublets or coats of arms appearing frequently. These are most often painted in blue, red, purple, orange, and green. All fighters wear closed helmets with visors that are illustrated quite uniformly; the amount of detail of the armour, on the other hand, varies considerably.

The weapons are drawn in a rather similar fashion as well, but the ecranches, the little shields, which mostly lie on the ground, are rendered a bit oddly: the bouche, the indentation for the spear or the lance,[17] is usually situated—in heraldic terms—on the right hand side of the shield. On folios 3r, 9v, 11r, 20r, 25r, 29r, and 41v, however, we find ecranches with a left sided orientation lying beneath or next to each of the left fighters; the same is true for the right fighters on folios 19v and 42r; the right one on fol. 4r is holding one of these in his hand; fol. 17r even portrays two wrongly arranged ecranches on the ground; and several ecranches seem to be devoid of any strap or grip at all: folios 9r, 14v, 15r, 15v, 16r, 16v, 17v, 18v, 19r, 20v, 21r, 23r, 23v, 26r, 26v, 27v, 28r, 28v, 31r, 31v, 34r, 36r, and 36v. With only a few exceptions, each ecranche displays a red St. George's cross on a white background.

Although the suits of armour vary considerably in detail, the overall style of the drawings appears homogeneous throughout, so that it is quite likely that only a single illustrator was responsible for the creation of the manuscript. In contrast to the Vienna *Gladiatoria* codex mentioned before, the pictures all share a similar high level of quality.

17 See also "Offence and Defence", p. 17.

Based on the particularities of the writing, the dialect, the arms, and the armour, the manuscript can be dated to about 1430.

Original Composition

Before the entire manuscript disappeared from Gotha, it consisted of three parts. The first one is the manuscript we deal with in this article; the second one is the fragment of a Spanish comedy, penned by Lope de Vega (1562–1635): *El testimonio vengado*; the third one remains lost without a trace to this day, and it contained several Spanish poems with later additions of French and Latin sentences on some leaves.[18]

That means that the original composition was as follows:

56 leaves of parchment:

- 1–43: *Gladiatoria Fechtbuch*
- 44: empty recto page, a pen sketch on the back
- 45–55: Lope de Vega: *El testimonio vengado*
- 56: title and listing of names

44 leaves of paper: Spanish poems, French and Latin texts

Regarding the correct number of pages, as for the question of format, a certain disagreement in the specialist literature prevails: Sometimes the number of parchment leaves is stated as 55, sometimes as 56. Quite probably, this inconsistency can be traced back to a mistake in counting the leaves that must have occurred even before the very first description of the manuscript written by Jacobs and Ukert. These two gentlemen account for 55 leaves, in which both Martin Wierschin[19] and Hans-Peter Hils[20] follow them. The latter first repeats Martin Wierschin's statement in *Meister Johann Liechtenauers Kunst des langen Schwertes*, but later on, in his essay from 1987 about three *Gladiatoria* manuscripts, he refers to the description of the manuscript by Rudolf Ehwald, director of the library in Gotha from 1893 until 1921, who counted 56 parchment leaves.[21] The *Katalog der deutschsprachigen illustrierten Handschriften des*

18 JACOBS/UKERT, loc. cit., p. 141.
19 WIERSCHIN: *Meister Johann Liechtenauers Kunst des Fechtens*, p. 17.
20 HILS: *Meister Johann Liechtenauers Kunst des langen Schwertes*, pp. 65.
21 EHWALD: *Chart. B 1974*. Gotha: Forschungsbibliothek, p. 164.

Mittelalters contains an internal discrepancy, since on one occasion it states 55, on another 56 leaves. Nevertheless, it points to a newer pagination only on the recto pages: 87–111. Cornelia Hopf lists 56 pages. The confusion can be explained quickly: Walter Benary[22] tells us in a footnote that page 101 (which corresponds to fol. 55) has been counted twice.

Benary reproduces the text of the fragment of the comedy in accordance with the original page numbers, namely from page 89 (fol. 45) to page 109 (fol. 55). In some additional remarks concerning the last part of the fragment he writes that fol. 55v (the verso page of the last leaf of our fragment) carries the name Pedro de l'Gurça; on fol. 56v there are some pen scribbles and the name Pedro dee Gnça (sic) in capital letters. Additionally, we find the title of the comedy on fol. 56r.[23]

The remaining leaf that belongs between the *Fechtbuch* and the fragment is blank on the recto page, and on fol. 44v (see plate 15) shows a rough pen sketch of a fighter in harness that is left uncoloured. The assumption that this drawing was executed by the writer of the comedy in the 17th century, using an illustration from the *Fechtbuch* as a template,[24] can certainly be excluded since neither the style of the depicted harness nor the combination of weapons—sword and dagger— appear in our manuscript in this manner.

22 Benary, loc. cit.

23 Hopf, loc. cit., p. 67.

24 *Katalog der deutschsprachigen illustrierten Handschriften des Mittelalters*, loc. cit.

II. LOCATIONS

Unfortunately, we cannot continuously verify the provenance of the manuscript; however, we can identify a number of locations that provide reliable indications regarding where it has been held.

Bavarian-Speaking Region

The manuscript came into being in the beginning of the 15th century, probably in the area of what today is Bavaria or Austria. It was presumably created in a larger studio or workshop, but only one scribe and one illustrator were involved.

Gotha

We can only trace back the history of the manuscript with certainty to the 18th century: Hereditary Prince August of Saxe-Gotha-Altenburg presented the volume to the Herzogliche Bibliothek Gotha (the ducal library) as a gift on October 22, 1792.

At this time, the manuscript *Membr. II 109* consisted of the aforementioned three parts. During or shortly after World War II, however, it disappeared from the library, only to resurface some time later and in separate parts:

The fragment of Lope de Vega's comedy was restored to the library in Gotha in 1997. This part had found its way into the possession of the antiquarian and auction house Hauswedell & Nolte in Hamburg, which handed it over to the Staats- und Universitätsbibliothek Hamburg (state and university library) in 1953 due to the unclear property situation. After an extensive examination, it was given back to the Forschungs- und Landesbibliothek Gotha.[25]

The third part remains lost to this day.

However, the first part, our *Fechtbuch*, reappeared in Heidelberg a couple of years after the end of the war.

25 Hopf, loc. cit., p. 67.

Heidelberg

The Buch- und Kunstantiquariat Dr. Helmut Tenner (book and art antiquarian) sold parts of the manuscript at several auctions in the 1950s and 60s. As far as we can determine, 19 individual leaves (out of 43) were sold at auction:[26]

Auction 5 on November 8/9, 1956: 3 leaves
Auction 7 on June 4/5, 1957: 4 leaves
Auction 9 on February 6–8, 1958: 4 leaves
Auction 11 on October 8/9, 1958: 6 leaves
Auction 37 on October 23/24, 1963: 1 leaf
Auction 43 on November 11/12, 1964: 1 leaf

Each auction catalogue depicts a manuscript page in a rough dot matrix print. We can definitely identify the images that are attached to Hans-Peter Hils' essay[27] as the ones stemming from the New Haven codex. Page and plate numbers in the corresponding auction catalogues are juxtaposed with the folio numbers of our manuscript in this table:

A5 (p. 4, no. 3): 28r
A7 (p. 5, no. 2): 34r
A9 (p. 3, no. 3): 9r
A11 (p. 2, no. 10 and plate 1): 30r
A37 (p. 5, no. 2): 22v
A43 (p. 5, no. 2 and plate 1): 18r

After this point, the line of descent is broken, and the fate of the remaining 24 leaves remains unresolved.

In fact, all of the sections that had been auctioned off at Tenner's—but obviously not only these—found their way to Sweden.

26 Hils: "Gladiatoria", loc. cit., pp. 11, 13.
27 Hils: "Gladiatoria", loc. cit., pp. 32–54.

Stockholm

AB Sandbergs Bokhandel in Stockholm sold the leaves that had been purchased at auction to the United States.

Paul Mellon

Paul Mellon (1907–99) was an American businessman, philanthropist and patron of the arts. He studied at Yale University in New Haven, Connecticut ,and was co-heir to a phenomenal fortune, that of the Mellon Bank, which was founded by his grandfather, father and uncle. He facilitated the foundation of the YCBA and made a vast number of charitable donations. Over the years, he purchased the entire *Gladiatoria Fechtbuch*:

1959: 28 leaves
February 1960: 11 leaves
December 1962: 2 leaves
December 1963: 1 leaf
December 1964: 1 leaf

Subsequently, the manuscript was put into the current order and re-bound by bookbinder Sven Wiklander.

New Haven, Connecticut

Paul Mellon bequeathed his collection, including our *Fechtbuch*, to the Rare Book and Manuscript Library (Paul Mellon Bequest) of the Yale Center for British Art, where it has resided since the time of his death.

III. THE EVIDENCE

In his 1985 general survey of German fencing manuscripts,[28] Hans-Peter Hils still lists the codex from Gotha and the so-called *manuscript 'T'* as two distinct volumes (catalogue nos. 21 and 23). But in 1987, he re-examined the descriptions of the manuscript and the catalogues of the Tenner auction house, and through a masterly investigative and deductive process, he came to the conclusion that these two were in fact one and the same book.[29]

In 2009, by using the various descriptions of the volume, I was finally able to identify the New Haven codex, which had become generally accessible in the meantime, as the manuscript that was believed to be lost.[30]

The criteria by which the codex that was presumed lost can be considered as rediscovered are these:

- The description of the manuscript and the text excerpt by Jacobs and Ukert.
- The description by Rudolf Ehwald.
- The documented list of some Spanish names on folio 43v.
- The plates in the auction catalogues.

1. Description by Jacobs and Ukert

Friedrich Jacobs and Friedrich August Ukert gave an account of a brief text passage in their description of the manuscript on page 9 (which corresponds to fol. 5r): "wenn du rasch den anderen packen willst, so nymb deinen speer und swert zw samb an den arm und schrawff ab den knoph von deinem swert und wirff heriklachen in in und lauff nach dem wurff mit ym ein und nutz swert oder spyes, welches dir eben sey. […] ob er also auf dich würff mit dem knoph, so nym dein taschen (Tartsche. Schild) für dich und vach darauff den Wurff und nym din spyes für dich in die recht hant zu dem stich und hüt dich sein dass er dir nicht inlauf, als er in synne hat."

28 Hils: *Meister Johann Liechtenauers Kunst des langen Schwertes*, p. 21–134.

29 Hils: "Gladiatoria", loc. cit.

30 I am very much indebted to Christian H. Tobler who was so kind as to draw my attention to this manuscript.

The transcription we offer in this book differs only slightly: “ob dw wildt reschleich mit ym entten So nymb deinen spyes vnd swert zw samb an den arm vnd schrawff ab den knöph von deinem swertt vnd wirff hertikchleichen in in vnd lauff nach dem würff mit ym ein vnd nütz swert oder spyes welichs dir eben sey ob er also auff dich wurff mit dem knopph So nym dein taschn für dich vnd vach darauff den wurff vnd nym den spyes für dich in die recht hant zw dem stich vnd rett dich sein das er dir nicht in lauff als er yndem synne hatt.”

Additionally, Jacobs and Ukert provide some details about certain pages that correspond to our manuscript: “From page 13 onwards combat goes on with the sword, from page 59 onwards with the dagger. On page 81 start depictions of how to hold the overthrown adversary.” The last two statements are accurate; the first one, however, is not. Page 13 corresponds to folio 7; sword fighting, though, already begins on fol. 5v. Nevertheless, this very page is marked with a number “13” written in ink, which does not relate to the actual page number, allowing us easily to explain this discrepancy.

2. Description by Ehwald

Rudolf Ehwald also provides us with several page and leaf numberings in his description of the codex, most of which closely approximate to those from the New Haven manuscript. Minor differences result in part from the new rebinding, in the process of which the original order was not entirely maintained: “On pages 3, 4, 8 the text beneath the picture is cut off. 2 leaves are missing in the beginning (= title and three pages with pictures), 1 leaf between 35 and 36, 6 leaves between 37 and 38, 1 leaf between 38 and 39, at least 1 leaf before 41. Leaves 1–6 are marked on the individual pages from a more recent hand on each page with 4–15, leaf 7 is unmarked, leaf 8 with the signature 16, 9–14 with later signatures 11–16; 15–17 unmarked; 18–23 have page numbers 22/25, 37=26, 39/43=31/36; in addition, however, leaves 30/37 possess the page numbers 1–12 [...], 15–18. Leaves 1, 2 describe the 4th to 7th, leaf 5r the 12th technique of spear fighting; leaves 30/35 eleven subsequent figures of dagger fighting; leaves 36, 37 the 14th/17th, leaf 38 the 30th/31st, leaves 39/40 the 34th/37th figures of the same fight; from the last series only pictures 3/7 have survived. Leaf 43 only has a picture on the front.”

Unfortunately, there are several difficulties with the above. On the one hand Rudolf Ehwald states that leaves 15 to 17 are unmarked. But this isn't so, at least not in the current order. In the reconstructed version which I present in table II (p. 239) in the appendix, there are even more unmarked pages. As such, this statement must remain in doubt.

On the other hand, he writes that the leaves 18–23 show the leaf numbers 22–25 (although not continuously). Yet these numbers are on leaves 29–32 and show the last of the wrestling techniques and the beginning of the dagger section. Elsewhere, Ehwald indicates eleven consecutive dagger techniques for leaves 30–35, which indeed corresponds to the facts. Unfortunately, this contradiction is also impossible to resolve.

Furthermore, he seems to have simply miscalculated when enumerating the "last series" of the holding down techniques, since the manuscript features five techniques out of seven, not three.

3. Spanish Names

Jacobs and Ukert wrote: "On the back of the last leaf a more recent hand has written down several names: Don Diego de Coes, Juan Perez del Gurca"; and Walter Benary said: "Various names are inscribed in the volume, which read as follows: fol. 43v (the verso of the last leaf of the *Fechtbuch*): Don Diego de Coes (twice). Juan Perez del Gurca. Jusepe Cerdeño." These are exactly the names we can find on fol. 43v of our *Fechtbuch* – although the Spanish researcher Manuel Valle Ortiz offers a somewhat different reading of the first two names: Sr Don Diego de Cea and Juan Perez de Quirça.

4. Plates

As already outlined above, the plates from the catalogues of the Tenner auction house clearly correspond to those from the New Haven manuscript, thus forming our most striking evidence.

Consequently, Hans-Peter Hils was able to prove as a first step that the codex from Gotha and the *manuscript 'T'* are one and the same book; and then, in a second step, I succeeded in verifying that this very manuscript is identical to that one from New Haven and therefore can no longer be considered lost at all.

IV. The Structure

Over the course of its history, the manuscript has been taken apart and rebound repeatedly. The current binding is incoherent and doesn't always follow a consistent order. Nevertheless, bookbinder Sven Wiklander has recognisably made great efforts to bring the pages into a logical and comprehensible order based on the above-mentioned diverse numberings. However, he did not succeed in every aspect, as we can see on folios 27r and 28v: As these two pages depict the sequence of a technique with the plate gauntlet, they clearly belong together, but are separated here. For a direct comparison, we can turn to the same sequence in the codex from Cracow on folios 26v and 27r, or 24v and 25r respectively in the Vienna version. Both codices preserve the correct order of the technique.

I have already indicated above the different numberings that occur throughout the manuscript. Subsequently, I will strive to use these and a number of additional descriptions and hints as a means to reconstruct the order the pages were in when the volume still resided in Gotha. I also attempt to reconstruct its original form—if there ever was one to begin with. For even Jacobs and Ukert wrote: "The bookbinder has not been mindful and has not sewn in the parchment leaves in their proper order; he has also damaged many a figure by cropping [the pages]."[31] As a guideline for this reconstruction, I have used the two *Gladiatoria* manuscripts from Cracow and Vienna which principally follow the same internal logic. Thus a theoretical original composition can be determined quite exactly.

Table I on page 236 shows the current state of the manuscript and lists all numberings. The most important criterion is the number of the individual *Stück* (or fighting technique) in the beginning. A slash "/" marks those pages whose text has been cut off. The techniques for spear and dagger fighting and for holding down are numbered throughout in the text; only for the sword is this not the case. Consequently, it is only here that the order of the pages has become confused.

31 Jacobs/Ukert: *Beiträge*, loc. cit.

Additionally, we have leaf numberings from the old days, but we cannot tell for sure whether these were allocated in the time or even in the process of the making of the manuscript, or at some later date. The nature and the style of the numbers point at least to the period of origin of the manuscript. The dagger techniques feature an old numbering as well, and the spear fighting section has been numbered in more recent times. The final, likewise not entirely universal page numbering in pencil was presumably done in the 1960s.

The last column of the table shows the order of the pages from the time in Gotha. Here the sequence is partially interrupted since unfortunately it proved to be impossible to determine the exact state. Those leaves that are shifted in contrast to the current order are marked red for reasons of clarification.

The *Stücke* in sword fighting are unnumbered in the New Haven and the Vienna manuscript, thus differing from the Cracow version. Nevertheless, there is frequently a definite order when a certain technique is followed by its corresponding counter technique. These passages are marked with small letters. Since the sequence of the manuscript was disrupted in the process of rebinding it, a certain technique is now followed by the wrong counter on several occasions. In order to clarify the original composition, sequences that belong together are marked with small Roman numerals. The order follows the codex from Cracow, which features a stringent numbering of the sword-fighting techniques.

Table II on page 239 offers the complete reconstructed proper sequence which is displayed in the first column on the basis of the current extent of the manuscript. The second column takes into consideration all page losses that can be demonstrated particularly by the numbering in the techniques directly in the text; missing passages are marked with square brackets. The third column repeats the numbering of the techniques as they occur in the text like in the second table in order to facilitate an enhanced comparison with the manuscripts from Vienna and Cracow. These two are also introduced with their respective foliation and sequence of techniques. It becomes apparent that none of the three *Gladiatoria* manuscripts is entirely complete; but, in sum, we are able to reconstruct an archetype. Thus we obtain an overview of not only the probable original sequence of the New Haven codex but also of the initial extent of the work, which must have included at least eleven additional leaves.

By means of these juxtapositions, it becomes evident that more than half of the manuscript was quite probably in the same order since the days of its creation. The consecutive numbering of the fencing techniques provides the most striking support for this position. Further considerations, however, must remain provisional, as they cannot be resolved unambiguously.

When we create a composition based on the two *Gladiatoria* manuscripts from Cracow and Vienna—as has been done in columns two and three in the second table—the following inconsistencies appear:

Leaf 7 is tricky to integrate in every regard. On one hand, its condition has suffered more than any other leaf; if, on the other hand, we insert it into the textually correct position, it is located between the current leaves 10 and 11, which were marked consecutively as 12 and 13 long ago. Thus, it doesn't really fit there. Furthermore, leaf 7 carries the number 16. There is another leaf in this manuscript with that same leaf number 16, namely leaf 14. But this is located in correct proximity to leaves 13 and 15—which carry the numbers 15 and 17. In order to complicate matters even more, leaves 25 and 15, which belong together as stated in the reconstructed order, carry the leaf numbers 15 and 17 respectively, so a leaf 16 might very well fit between them. The handwriting of the numbering, however, shows a thoroughly distinct character.

When we turn our attention more closely to the old foliation from 11–16, we realise that the reconstructed tenth leaf (currently leaf 9) shows the folio number 11.

A consideration: when the foliation was being executed, which stylistically fits very well into the period of origin of the codex, leaf 7 (the dirty one) had already been inserted wrongly, namely before the *original* tenth leaf, so that it was counted as the eleventh one. Thus the sequence of the leaves of the manuscript may have been disrupted even at the time of its creation.

A daring hypothesis: what if the author of our *Fechtbuch* had noticed this erroneous composition completed by a bookbinder who was not familiar with the correct execution of the fencing techniques—albeit too late—and subsequently proceeded also to number the sword-fighting techniques in the text itself, as he had done with the remaining spear, dagger, and holding-down techniques in any case? In this way, he could prevent further discrepancies in future editions of the *Gladiatoria* corpus. And indeed, the sword-fighting techniques are in fact numbered in the text of the Cracow version that was created later.

Beyond that, the sequence of leaf numbering from 15 to 36, that presumably was written by one scribe, remains a mystery, as it is interrupted by a larger block not only in the reconstructed version but also in the present one.

There also remains some uncertainty with regard to leaf 20. In contrast to the two *Gladiatoria* manuscripts from Cracow and Vienna, the order of both pages is reversed.

Nevertheless, writing in response to my inquiry, Francis Lapka said that he could not find any clue to prove that the leaf had been inserted the wrong way round: "The inner margin is still rather healthy in breadth, while the outer margin is closely trimmed (with minor loss of content, as with other leaves in the volume)." If the page was ever reversed, this must have happened a long time before the most recent rebinding.

Ultimately, we end up with several possibilities for assembling the manuscript by making use of the various available numberings; unfortunately, none of them turns out to be entirely coherent. Even the continuous page numbers don't lead to satisfying and convincing results: if we kept together the old numbered leaves 21 and 22, we would pull apart the aforementioned connected sequence of the technique with the plate gauntlet (ff. 28v and 27r). In the end, the foliations and paginations that stem from different times can only serve as reference points. It is unlikely that we can ever know the initial structure of the manuscript with certainty.

Regarding the equally incomplete modern pagination in pencil, the odds are that the four leaves without that pagination (11, 18, 22 and 26) were the last ones that Paul Mellon purchased between 1962 and 1964, meaning that the pagination must have been done between February 1960 and December 1962. Another theory brought forward by Dr. Elisabeth Fairman, curator of the manuscript library of the YCBA, is that the three leaves with the cut-off texts were the last ones to be purchased—which unfortunately does not coincide very well with the actual leaf numbers. Since we regrettably cannot determine when Paul Mellon acquired each leaf, this question must also remain unsettled.

The long-lost fencing manuscript has resurfaced, yet it stubbornly refuses to give up its last secrets.

TABLES

I.

Present and Gotha State

Folio	Piece	Leaf	Page, old	Page, new	Pencil	Other	Gotha
SPEAR							
1r	4			4	1		1r
1v	5			5	2		1v
2r	6			6	3		2r
2v	7		7 (?)	7	4		2v
3r	/			8	5		3r
3v	/			9	6		3v
4r	/			10	7		4r
4v	/			11	8		4v
5r	12			12	9		5r
SWORD							
5v	Be-gin-ning			13	10		5v
6r				14	11		6r
6v				15	12	15 (?)[1]	6v
7r	/ [i a]			6 (?)	13	16	8r
7v	/ [i b]				14		8v
8r					15		7r
8v					16		7v
9r		11			17		9r
9v					18		9v
10r		12			19		10r
10v					20		10v
11r	ii a	13					11r
11v	ii b						11v
12r	iii a	14			21		12r
12v	iii b				22		12v

Folio	Piece	Leaf	Page, old	Page, new	Pencil	Other	Gotha
13r		15			23		13r
13v	iv a				24		13v
14r	iv b	16			25		14r
14v	iv c				26		14v
15r	vii a	17			27		
15v	vii b				28		
16r	vii c	18			29		
16v	viii a				30		
17r	viii b	19			31		
17v	ix a				32		
18r	ix b	20					
18v	x a						
19r	xiii a				33		
19v	xiii b				34		
20r					35		
20v					36		
21r					37		
21v					38		
22r	xii b					2^2	
22v							
23r					39		
23v					40		
24r	v b				41		
24v	vi a				42		
25r	vi b	15			43		
25v					44		
26r							
26v	v a						
27r	xi b				45		
27v	xii a				46		

Folio	Piece	Leaf	Page, old	Page, new	Pencil	Other	Gotha
28r	x b	21			47		
28v	xi a				48		
29r		22			49		
29v					50		
DAGGER							
30r	1[3]	23	1		51		30r
30v	2		2		52		30v
31r	2	24	3		53		31r
31v	3		4		54		31v
32r	4	25	5		55		32r
32v	5		6		56		32v
33r	6		7		57		33r
33v	7		8		58		33v
34r	8		9		59		34r
34v	9		10		60		34v
35r	10		11		61		35r
35v	11		12		62		35v
36r	14		15		63		36r
36v	15		16		64		36v
37r	16	26	17		65		37r
37v	17		18		66		37v
38r	30				67		38r
38v	31				68		38v
39r	34	31			69		39r
39v	35				70		39v
40r	36	32			71		40r
40v					72		40v
HOLDING DOWN							
41r	3	34			73		41r
41v	4				74		41v

Folio	Piece	Leaf	Page, old	Page, new	Pencil	Other	Gotha
42r	5	35			75		42r
42v	6				76		42v
43r	7	36			77		43r

II.

Reconstructed Version

New Haven			Vienna		Cracow	
Original	Adjusted	Piece	Folio	Piece	Folio	Piece
			SPEAR			
	[1r]				1r	Title
	[1v]	[1]			1v	1
	[2r]	[2]	1r	2	2r	2
	[2v]	[3]	1v	3	2v	3
1r	3r	4	2r	4	3r	4
1v	3v	5	2v	5	3v	5
2r	4r	6	3r	6	4r	6
2v	4v	7	3v	7	4v	7
3r	5r	[8]	4r	8	5r	8
3v	5v	[9]	4v	9	5v	9
4r	6r	[10]	5r	10	6r	10
4v	6v	[11]	5v	11	6v	11
5r	7r	12	6r	12	7r	12
			SWORD			
5v	7v	Beginning	6v	Beginning	7v	Beginning
					8r	1/1[4]

New Haven			Vienna		Cracow	
Original	Adjusted	Piece	Folio	Piece	Folio	Piece
					8v	1/2[4]
6r	8r		7r		9r	2
6v	8v		7v		9v	3
8r	9r		8r		10r	4
8v	9v		8v		10v	5
9r	10r		9r		11r	6
9v	10v		9v		11v	7
10r	11r		10r		12r	8
10v	11v		10v		12v	9
7r	12r	[i a]	11r	i a	13r	10 i a
7v	12v	[i b]	11v	i b	13v	11 i b
11r	13r	ii a	12r	ii a	14r	12 ii a
11v	13v	ii b	12v	ii b	14v	13 ii b
12r	14r	iii a	13r	iii a	15r	14 iii a
12v	14v	iii b	13v	iii b	15v	15 iii b
13r	15r		14r		16r	16
13v	15v	iv a	14v	iv a	16v	17 iv a
14r	16r	iv b	15r	iv b	17r	18 iv b
14v	16v	iv c	15v	iv c	17v	19 iv c
23r	17r		16r		18r	20
23v	17v		16v		18v	21
26r	18r		17r		19r	22
26v	18v	v a	17v	v a	19v	23 v a
24r	19r	v b	18r	v b	20r	24 v b
24v	19v	vi a	18v	vi a	20v	25 vi a
					21r	26 vi b
25r	20r	vi b	19r	vi b		
25v	20v		19v		21v	27
15r	21r	vii a	20r	vii a	22r	28 vii a

New Haven			Vienna		Cracow	
Original	Adjusted	Piece	Folio	Piece	Folio	Piece
15v	21v	vii b	20v	vii b	22v	29 vii b
16r	22r	vii c	21r	vii c	23r	30 vii c
16v	22v	viii a	21v	viii a	23v	31 viii a
17r	23r	viii b	22r	viii b	24r	32 viii b
17v	23v	ix a	22v	ix a	24v	33 ix a
18r	24r	ix b	23r	ix b	25r	34 ix b
18v	24v	x a	23v	x a	25v	35 x a
28r	25r	x b	24r	x b	26r	36 x b
28v	25v	xi a	24v	xi a	26v	37 xi a
27r	26r	xi b	25r	xi b	27r	xi b
27v	26v	xii a	25v	xii a	27v	39 xii a
22r	27r	xii b	26r	xii b	28r	40 xii b
22v	27v		26v		28v	41
19r	28r	xiii a	27r	xiii a	29r	42 xiii a
19v	28v	xiii b	27v	xiii b	29v	43 xiii b
20v[5]	29r (?)		28r	xiv a	30r	44 xiv a
			28v	xiv b	30v	45 xiv b
20r[5]	29v (?)		29r		31r	46
21r	30r		29v		31v	47
21v	30v		30r		32r	48
29r	31r		30v		32v	49
29v	31v		31r		33r	50
DAGGER						
30r	32r	1[3]	31v	[6]		
30v	32v	2	32r	1	33v	1
31r	33r	2	32c	2	34r	2
31v	33v	3	33r	3	34v	3
32r	34r	4	33v	4	35r	4
32v	34v	5	34r	5	35v	5

New Haven			Vienna		Cracow	
Original	Adjusted	Piece	Folio	Piece	Folio	Piece
33r	35r	6	34v	6	36r	6
33v	35v	7	35r	7	36v	7
34r	36r	8	35v	8	37r	8
34v	36v	9	36r	9	37v	9
35r	37r	10	36v	10	38r	10
35v	37v	11	37r	11	38v	11
	[38r]	[12]	37v	12	39r	12
	[38v]	[13]	38r	13	39v	13
36r	39r	14	38v	14	40r	14
36v	39v	15	39r	15	40v	15
37r	40r	16	39v	16	41r	16
37v	40v	17	40r	17	41v	17
	[41r]	[18]	40v	18	42r	18
	[41v]	[19]	41r	19	42v	19
	[42r]	[20]	41v	20	43r	20
	[42v]	[21]	42r	21	43v	21
	[43r]	[22]	42v	22		[22]
	[43v]	[23]	43r	23		[23]
	[44r]	[24]	43v	24		[24]
	[44v]	[25]	44r	25		[25]
	[45r]	[26]	44v	26	44r	26
	[45v]	[27]	45r[7]	27	44v[7]	27
	[46r]	[28]	45v	28	45r	28
	[46v]	[29]	46r	29	45v	29
38r	47r	30	46v	30	46r	30
38v	47v	31	47r	31	46v	31
	[48r]	[32]	47v	32	47r	32
	[48v]	[33]	48r	33	47v	33
39r	49r	33	48v	34	48r	34
39v	49v	35	49r	[6]	48v	35

New Haven			Vienna		Cracow	
Original	Adjusted	Piece	Folio	Piece	Folio	Piece
40r	50r	36	49v[8]	[6]		
40v	50v		53r		49r[9]	36
HOLDING DOWN						
	[51r]	[1]	53v	1	56r	1
	[51v]	[2]	54r	2	56v	2
41r	52r	3	54v	3	57r	3
41v	52v	4	55r	4	57v	4
42r	53r	5	55v	5	58r	5
42v	53v	6	56r	6	58v	6
43r	54r	7	56v	7	59r	7

1 Difficult to decipher; may be a second 15.
2 In pencil, circled.
3 *Gladiatoria* Cracow doesn't contain the first dagger technique at all while in Vienna, the image exists, but the text is missing. This means that the numbering of the pieces in New Haven should be one greater throughout the codex when compared to the other two versions. However, starting with the third piece, the "regular" numbering is maintained and corresponds to the other two manuscripts.
4 This technique is explained on two pages.
5 In contrast to the two *Gladiatoria* manuscripts from Cracow and Vienna the order of these pages is reversed.
6 Without text.
7 The texts are identical, the images differ.
8 Followed by three empty leaves in the manuscript from Vienna.
9 Fols 49v–55v show a variety of unarmoured fencing disciplines, such as fighting with the staff, sword and buckler, or the large duelling shield.

PLATES

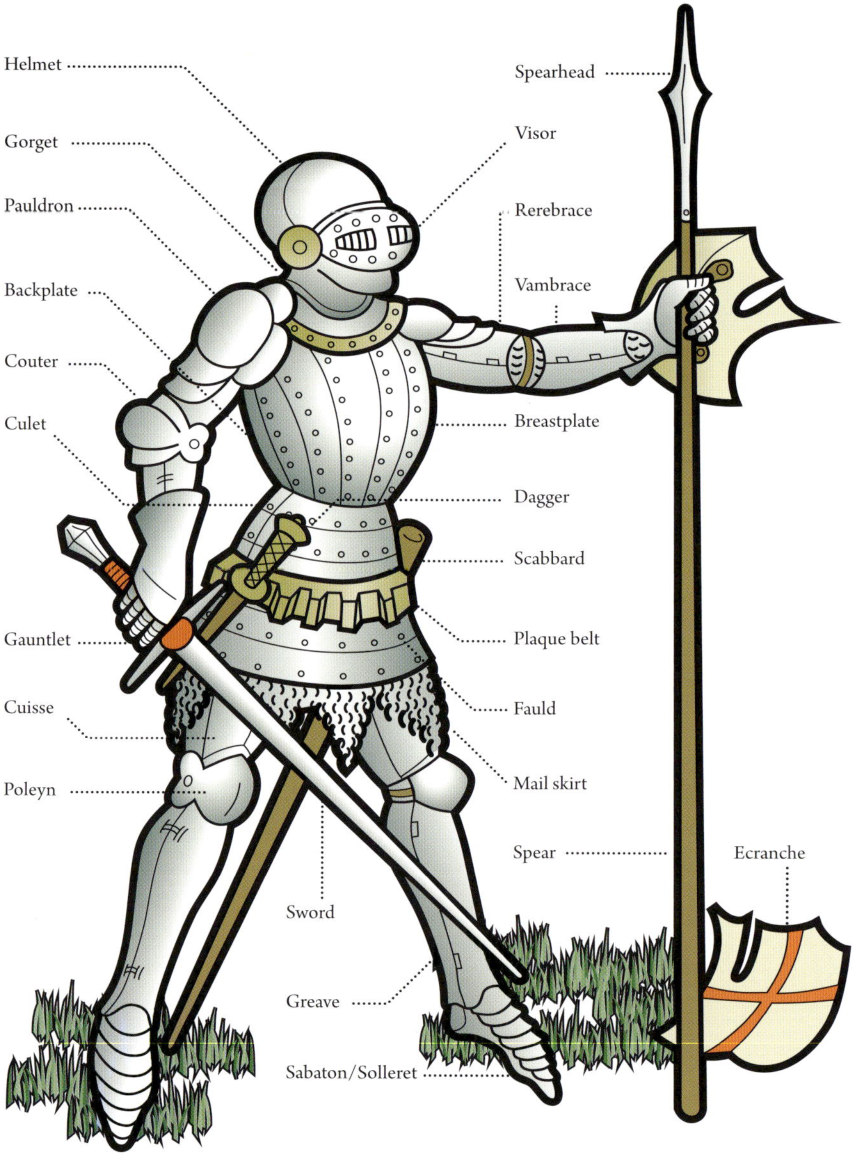

1 *The harness and its components.*
© Dierk Hagedorn

2 *Early Italian harness from the Churburg armoury.*
© Churburg, Schluderns

3 *A composite Kastenbrust harness from the Wien Museum in Vienna.*

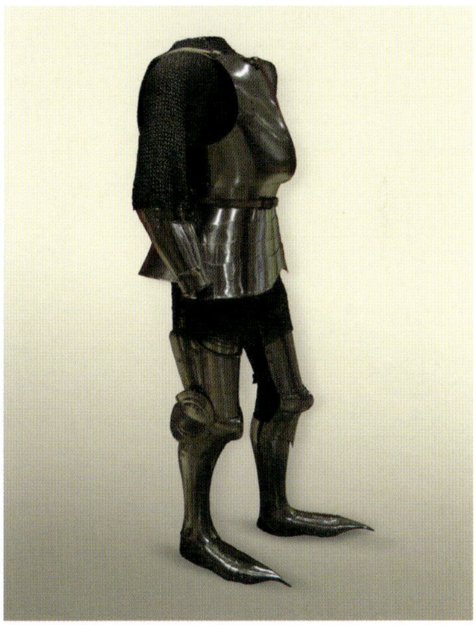

4 *Rogier van der Weyden: Saint George and the Dragon, 1432–35. © Washington, National Gallery of Art, Ailsa Mellon Bruce Fund*

5 *St. George from the high altar of St. George's church in Wismar, about 1430. © Wismar, St. Nikolaikirche*

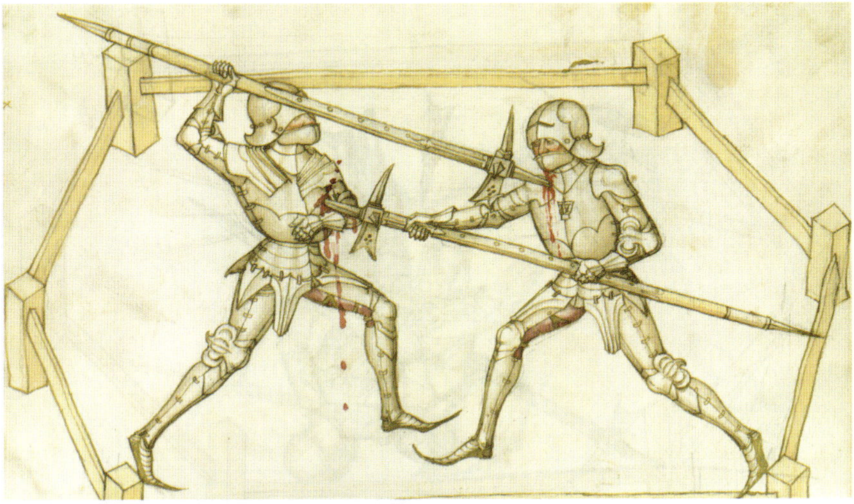

6 *Hans Talhoffer: Harness fencing with the pollaxe, Thott 290 2o, fol. 134v.*
© København, Det Kongelige Bibliotek

7 *Armoured combat with fatal consequences in the so-called codex Manesse, Cod. Pal. germ. 848, fol. 321v.*
© Universitätsbibliothek Heidelberg

8 *Cod. Guelf. 78.2 Aug. 20, fol. 94v.*
© Wolfenbüttel, Herzog August-Bibliothek

9 *Cod. Guelf. 78.2 Aug. 2°, fol. 109v.*
© Wolfenbüttel, Herzog August-Bibliothek

10 *Cod. Guelf. 78.2 Aug. 2°, fol. 34r.*
© Wolfenbüttel, Herzog August-Bibliothek

11 *Cod.I.6.4°.2, fol. 82v.*
© Augsburg, Universitätsbibliothek

12 *Paulus Kal, Cgm 1507, fol. 19r. © Bayerische Staatsbibliothek München*

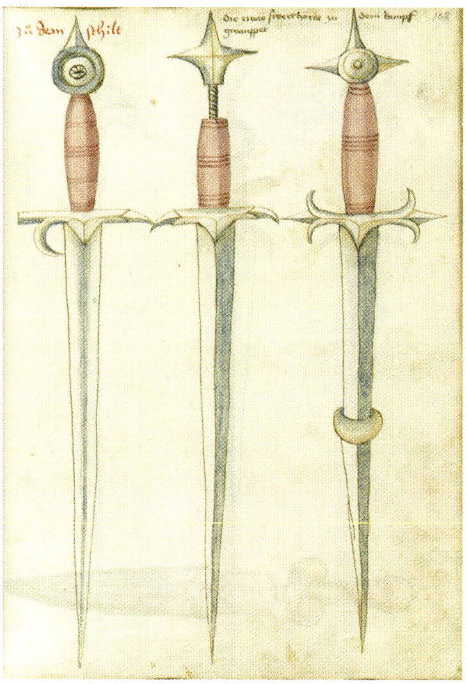

13 *Hans Talhoffer, Thott 290 2°, fol. 108r. © København, Det Kongelige Bibliotek*

14 *Hans Talhoffer, Thott 290 2°, fol. 107v. © København, Det Kongelige Bibliotek*

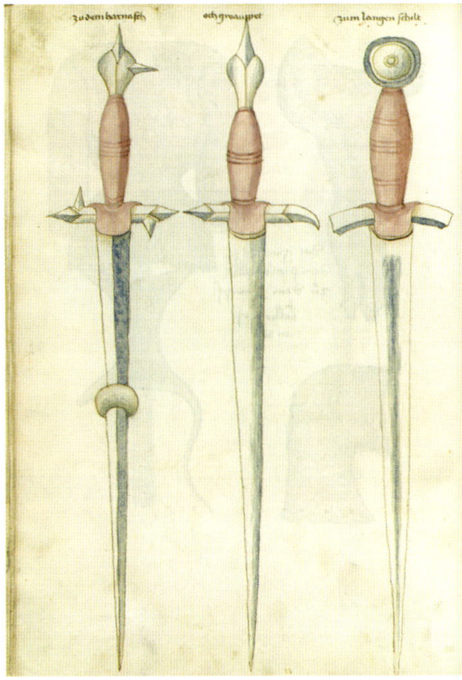

15 *Memb. II 109, fol. 44v. © Forschungsbibliothek Gotha der Universität Erfurt*

GLOSSARY

GLOSSARY

Ansetzen *(Setting the point, lodging the point)*: The action of successfully placing the point of your sword on the target, but not yet penetrating it or causing injury to your opponent. A common tactical situation with many counter techniques.

Arbait *(Work)*: Any action that attempts to harm or incapacitate the opponent.

Ausserhalb *(Outside)*: Refers to an attack or action that comes to the right side of the sword (looking from the defender's point of view) or towards the back side.

Bruch *(Break, a counter)*: A counter of a given piece or technique.

Dringen an die Prust *(Pressing on the breast)*: An action of setting the point (→*Ansetzen*) on the breast or under the armpit of your opponent and pushing him to leave the field of battle or injure him. A common tactical situation with many counter techniques.

Durch *(Through)*: Describes the movement that starts on one side (e. g. inside), and ends on the other side (e. g. outside).

Halten *(Holding)*: Techniques for immobilising or incapacitating your opponent while fighting on the ground. Also called →*Unterhalten*.

Innerhalb *(Inside)*: Refers to an attack or action to the left of the sword (from the defender's point of view), between the body and the sword.

Kurtzes schwert *(Shortened sword)*: One of the terms used to describe fighting in armour when the sword is grabbed with the left hand in the middle of the blade.

Mordslag *(Murder strike)*: Striking with the pommel—the left hand grabs the middle of the blade, and the right hand the point, effectively turning the sword into a small pollaxe.

Ringen *(Wrestling)*: Unarmed combat. In armour, this generally means throwing, unbalancing or using leverage to immobilize your opponent or bring him to the ground.

Scher *(Scissors)*: A counter against the attempt to resolve the impasse of both opponents grabbing each other's swords by turning underneath the blades. Its name comes from the crossing of the two swords over the opponent's body, which resembles the action of scissors.

Strass der Glider ***(Way of the joints)*****:** A set of pieces which rely on very strong leverage against a wrist or an elbow.

Stuckh ***(Piece)*****:** A set of movements and actions of both opponents, which has a distinct beginning and generally ends with the incapacitation of the opponent or retreat.

Unterhalten ***(Holding on the ground)*****:** See →*Halten.*

Versetzen ***(Parry)*****:** A defensive action of stopping an attack with the blade by interception or displacement.

Wag ***(Scales)*****:** Balanced wrestling position with bent knees to keep the centre of gravity low.

Wiederbruch ***(The counter's counter)*****:** The counter to a counter of a given piece or technique.

BIBLIOGRAPHY

BIBLIOGRAPHY

I.
Manuscripts of the *Gladiatoria* Group (in Order of Repository)

Cod.I.6.4°.2 (Codex Wallerstein). Augsburg: Universitätsbibliothek

Ms. Berol. germ. quart. 16. Cracow: Biblioteka Jagiellońska

MS U860.F46 1450. New Haven, Connecticut, Yale Center for British Art

CL23842. Paris: Musée National du Moyen Âge

KK 5013. Vienna: Kunsthistorisches Museum

Cod Guelf. 78.2 Aug. 2°. Wolfenbüttel: Herzog August-Bibliothek

II.
Manuscripts with Illustrated Fighting Techniques in Harness (in Order of Repository)

Anton Rast: *Schätze 82 Reichsstadt.* Augsburg: Stadtarchiv

Hans Talhoffer: *Cod.I.6.2°.1.* Augsburg: Universitätsbibliothek

Jörg Wilhalm: *Cod.I.6.4°.5.* Augsburg: Universitätsbibliothek

Jörg Wilhalm: *Cod.I.6.2°.3.* Augsburg: Universitätsbibliothek

Hans Talhoffer: *78 A 15.* Berlin: Kupferstichkabinett der Stiftung Preußischer Kulturbesitz

Anonymous: *Libr. pict. A 83.* Berlin: Staatsbibliothek Preußischer Kulturbesitz

Paulus Kal: *Ms. 1825.* Bologna: Biblioteca Universitaria

Hans Talhoffer: *Thott 290 2°.* Copenhagen: Det Kongelige Bibliotek

Fiore dei Liberi: *Flos Duellatorum.* Corbetta: Museo archeologico Villa Pisani Dossi

Paulus Hector Mair: *Mscr. Dresd. C.93/94.* Dresden: Sächsische Landesbibliothek

LUDWIG (VI.) VON EYB ZUM HARTENSTEIN: *B 26*. Erlangen: Universitätsbibliothek

HANS TALHOFFER: *Philos. 61*. Göttingen: Niedersächische Staats- und Universitätsbibliothek

PAULUS KAL: *Ms. Chart. B1021*. Gotha: Forschungsbibliothek Schloss Friedenstein

HANS TALHOFFER: *Ms. Chart. A 558*. Gotha: Forschungsbibliothek Schloss Friedenstein

HANS CZYNNER: *MS. 963*. Graz: Universitätsbibliothek

ANONYMOUS: *2° Ms. Math. 7*. Kassel: Landesbibliothek

HANS TALHOFFER: *Hs. XIX, 17–3*. Königseggwald: Gräfliches Schloss

FIORE DEI LIBERI: *MS Ludwig XV 13 (Fior di Battaglia)*. Los Angeles: J. Paul Getty Museum

PAULUS KAL: *Cgm 1507*. Munich: Bayerische Staatsbibliothek

PAULUS HECTOR MAIR: *Cod. icon. 393*. Munich: Bayerische Staatsbibliothek

HANS TALHOFFER: *Cod. icon. 394a*. Munich: Bayerische Staatsbibliothek

HANS TALHOFFER: *Cod. icon. 394*. Munich: Bayerische Staatsbibliothek

HANS TALHOFFER: *Cod. icon. 395*. Munich: Bayerische Staatsbibliothek

JÖRG WILHALM: *Cgm 3711*. Munich: Bayerische Staatsbibliothek

JÖRG WILHALM: *Cgm 3712*. Munich: Bayerische Staatsbibliothek

HANS TALHOFFER: *26.236*. New York: Metropolitan Museum of Art

FIORE DEI LIBERI: *B1.370.A MS M.0383 (Fior di Battaglia)*. New York: Morgan Library & Museum

FIORE DEI LIBERI: *MS Latin 11269 (Florius de Arte Luctandi)*. Paris: Bibliothèque Nationale de France

PHILIPPO DI VADI: *Cod.1324*. Rome: Biblioteca nazionale centrale di Roma

PAULUS KAL: *S554*. Solothurn: Zentralbibliothek

PETER FALKNER: *KK 5012*. Vienna: Kunsthistorisches Museum

PAULUS KAL: *KK 5126*. Vienna: Kunsthistorisches Museum

HANS TALHOFFER: *KK 5342*. Vienna: Kunsthistorisches Museum

FIORE DEI LIBERI: *Cod. 5278*. Vienna: Österreichische Nationalbibliothek

ANONYMOUS: *Cod. 10799*. Vienna, Österreichische Nationalbibliothek

ANONYMOUS: *Cod. Vindob. B 11093*. Vienna, Österreichische Nationalbibliothek

PAULUS HECTOR MAIR: *Cod. Vindob. 10825/6*. Vienna: Österreichische Nationalbibliothek

Lienhart Sollinger: *Cod. Guelf. 38.21 Aug. 2°.* Wolfenbüttel: Herzog August-Bibliothek

Hans Talhoffer: *Cod. Guelf. 125.16 Extrav.* Wolfenbüttel: Herzog August-Bibliothek

III.

Additional Manuscripts and Prints with Fighting Techniques in Harness (in Order of Repository)

Jude Lew: *Cod. I.6.4°.3.* Augsburg: Universitätsbibliothek

Anonymous: *Ms. germ. quart. 2020 (Goliath).* Cracow: Biblioteka Jagiellońska

Sigmund Ringeck: *Mscr. Dresd. C487.* Dresden: Sächsische Landesbibliothek

Anonymous: *E.1939.65.341.* Glasgow: R. L. Scott Collection

Gregor Erhart: *E.1939.65.354.* Glasgow: R. L. Scott Collection

Anonymous: *Cod. Hs. 3227a.* Nuremberg: Germanisches Nationalmuseum

Anonymous: *MS Francais 1996 (Le Jeu de la Hache).* Paris: Bibliothèque Nationale de France

Anonymous: *44 A 8 (Peter von Danzig).* Rome: Biblioteca dell'Accademia Nazionale dei Lincei e Corsiniana

Joachim Meyer: *Mss. var. 82.* Rostock: Universitätsbibliothek

Hans von Speyer: *M.I.29.* Salzburg: Universitätsbibliothek

Hans Folz: *Q 566.* Weimar: Nationale Forschungs- und Gedenkstätten der klassischen Deutschen Literatur in Weimar – Zentralbibliothek der deutschen Klassik

Monte, Pietro: *Exercitiorum Atque Artis Militaris Collectanea.* Milan: Giovani Angelo Scinzenzler, 1509

IV.
Monographs

Anglo, Sydney: *The Martial Arts of Renaissance Europe.* New Haven, London: Yale University Press, 2000

Bauer, Matthias Johannes: *Langes Schwert und Schweinespieß.* Graz: Akademische Druck- und Verlagsanstalt, 2009

Beaufort-Spontin, Christian/Pfaffenbichler, Matthias: *Meisterwerke der Hofjagd- und Rüstkammer.* Vienna: Kunsthistorisches Museum, 2005

Blair, Claude: *European Armour.* London: B. T. Batsford, 1958, reprinted 1972

Blair, Claude/Boccia, Lionello G./Fahy, Everett/Nickel, Helmut/Norman, A.V. B./Pyhrr, Stuart W./La Rocca, Donald J.: *Studies in European Arms and Armor.* Philadelphia: Philadelphia Museum of Art, 1992

Boccia, Lionello Giorgio: *Le armature di S. Maria delle Grazie di Curtatone di Mantova e l'armatura lombarda del '400.* Busto Arsizio: Bramante Editrice, 1982

Bodemer, Heidemarie: *Das Fechtbuch.* Institut für Kunstgeschichte, 2008

Boeheim, Wendelin: *Handbuch der Waffenkunde.* Leipzig: E. A. Seemann, 1890

Capwell, Tobias: *Masterpieces of European Arms and Armour in the Wallace Collection.* London: Paul Holberton Publishing, 2011

Capwell, Tobias: *The Noble Art of the Sword.* London: Paul Holberton Publishing, 2012

Capwell, Tobias: *The Real Fighting Stuff – Arms and Armour at Glasgow Museums.* Glasgow: Glasgow City Council Museums, 2007

Dobson, Christopher: *Alla Tedesca? Italian 'Gothic' Armour and the Export Trade.* Clare: Arms and Armour eBooks, 2012

Dufty, Arthur Richard: *European Armour in the Tower of London.* London: Her Majesty's Stationery Office, 1968

Edge, David/Paddock, John Miles: *Arms & Armor of the Medieval Knight: An Illustrated History of Weaponry in the Middle Ages.* Greenwich, Connecticut: Brompton Books, 1988

Fehr, Hans: *Der Zweikampf.* Berlin: Karl Curtius, 1908

Ffoulkes, Charles: *The Armourer and his Craft from the xi^th^ to the xvi^th^ Century.* London: Methuen, 1912

FLIEGEL, STEPHEN N.: *Arms and Armor: The Cleveland Museum of Art.* New York: Harry N. Abrams

FORGENG, JEFFREY L.: *The Medieval Art of Swordsmanship.* Union City, California: Chivalry Bookshelf, 2003

FRÜHMORGEN-VOSS, HELLA/OTT, NORBERT H./BODEMANN, ULRIKE/STÖLLINGER-LÖSER, CHRISTINE/LENG, RAINER (ED.): *Katalog der deutschsprachigen illustrierten Handschriften des Mittelalters* Band 4/2, Lfg. 1/2: 38. *Fecht- und Ringbücher.* Munich: Bayerische Akademie der Wissenschaften, 2009

FUNCKEN, LILIANE & FRED: *Historische Waffen und Rüstungen.* Niedernhausen: Orbis, 2001

GIESSAUF, JOHANNES/BERGNER, UTE: *Würgegriff und Mordschlag: Die Fecht- und Ringlehre des Hans Czynner (1538).* Graz: Akademische Druck- und Verlagsanstalt, 2005

GOLL, MATTHIAS: *Mit eiserner Faust.* Norderstedt: Books on Demand, 2009

GRAVETT, CHRISTOPHER: *German Medieval Armies 1300–1500.* London: Osprey, 1985

GRAVETT, CHRISTOPHER: *English Medieval Armies 1400–1500.* Oxford: Osprey, 2001

HAGEDORN, DIERK: *Peter von Danzig – Transkription und Übersetzung der Handschrift 44 A 8.* Herne: VS-Books, 2008

HILS, HANS-PETER: *Meister Johann Liechtenauers Kunst des langen Schwertes.* Frankfurt am Main: Verlag Peter Lang, 1985

HOPF, CORNELIA: *Die abendländischen Handschriften der Forschungs- und Landesbibliothek Gotha. Bestandsverzeichnis. 2. Kleinformatige Pergamenthandschriften Memb. II.* Gotha: Forschungs- und Landesbibliothek, 1997

HUHLE, HENNER/BRUNCK, HELMA: *500 Jahre Fechtmeister in Deutschland. Ältester privilegierter Berufsstand.* Kelkheim im Taunus: Kunz, 1987,

HULL, JEFFREY: *Knightly Dueling: The Fighting Arts of German Chivalry.* Boulder, Colorado: Paladin Press, 2008

JACOBS, FRIEDRICH/UKERT, FRIEDRICH AUGUST: *Beiträge zur ältern Litteratur oder Merkwürdigkeiten der Herzogl. öffentlichen Bibliothek zu Gotha, Fünftes Heft oder dritten Bandes erstes Heft.* Leipzig: Dyk'sche Buchhandlung, 1838

Jaquet, Daniel: *Combattre en armure à la fin du Moyen Âge et au début de la Renaissance d'après l'étude des livres de combat*, Ph.D dissertation. History Department, University of Geneva, 2013

Jaquet, Daniel (ed.): *L'art chevaleresque du combat*. Neuchâtel: Éditions Alphil-Presses universitaires suisses, 2012

Kappelmayr, Barbara/Meier, Andreas: *Ms. B 26, Ludwig (VI.) v. Eyb zum Hartenstein*. Gesellschaft für pragmatische Schriftlichkeit, 2010

Klučina, Petr: *Rüstungen*. Hanau: Werner Dausien, 1993

Kohlmorgen, Jan: *Der mittelalterliche Reiterschild*. Wald-Michelbach: Karfunkel-Verlag, 2002

Königsegg-Aulendorf, Johannes Graf zu/Schulze, André: *Der Königsegger Codex*. Mainz: Philipp von Zabern, 2010

Kühnel, Harry (ed.): *Bildwörterbuch der Kleidung und Rüstung*. Stuttgart: Alfred Körner Verlag, 1992

Laible, Thomas: *Das Schwert. Mythos und Wirklichkeit*. Bruckmühl: Wieland Verlag, 2006

Laking, Guy Francis: *A Record of European Armour and Arms through Seven Centuries*, Vol. II. London: G. Bell and Sons, 1920

Lanzardo, Dario (ed.): *Ritter-Rüstungen*. Munich: Callwey, 1990

Lauts, Jan: *Alte deutsche Waffen*. Burg b. M.: August Hopfer, 1938

Lehnart, Ulrich: *Kleidung & Waffen der Früh- und Hochgotik – 1150–1320*. Wald-Michelbach: Karfunkel-Verlag, 2001

Lehnart, Ulrich: *Kleidung & Waffen der Spätgotik I, 1320–1370*. Wald-Michelbach: Karfunkel-Verlag, 2000

Lehnart, Ulrich: *Kleidung & Waffen der Spätgotik II, 1370–1420*. Wald-Michelbach: Karfunkel-Verlag, 2003

Lehnart, Ulrich: *Kleidung & Waffen der Spätgotik III, 1420–1480*. Wald-Michelbach: Karfunkel-Verlag, 2005

Leoni, Tom: *Fiore de' Liberi's Fior di Battaglia. M.S. Getty Ludwig XV 13*. Lulu.com, 2009

Lorbeer, Carsten: *Transkription von KK 5013*. Gesellschaft für pragmatische Schriftlichkeit, 2006

Lorbeer, Carsten/Lorbeer, Julia/Meier, Andreas/Wiedner, Marita/Heim, Johann: *Edition zu den Handschriften Paulus Kals*. Gesellschaft für pragmatische Schriftlichkeit, 2006

LORBEER, CARSTEN/LORBEER, JULIA/ GIESSL, ALEX/KAPPELMAYR, BARBARA/BRUNNER, ROBERT/FREUNDL, MARION/WIEDNER, MARITA/MEIER, ANDREAS/BABIC, KRISTIAN: *Transkription von Ms. germ. quart. 16.* Gesellschaft für pragmatische Schriftlichkeit, 2006

MARTIN, PAUL: *Waffen und Rüstungen von Karl dem Großen bis zu Ludwig XIV.* Frankfurt: Umschau Verlag, 1967

MEIER, ANDREAS/WIEDNER, MARITA: *Transkription der Handschrift Hs. Best. 7020 des Historischen Archivs der Stadt Köln.* Gesellschaft für pragmatische Schriftlichkeit, 2007

MICHAELI, VIGO VON: *Schöne alte Waffen und Rüstungen.* Bayreuth: Gondrom, 1979

MONDSCHEIN, KEN: *The Knightly Art of Battle.* Los Angeles: Getty Publications, 2011

MÜLLER, HEINRICH/KUNTER, FRITZ: *Europäische Helme.* Berlin: Militärverlag der Deutschen Demokratischen Republik, 1984

MÜLLER, HEINRICH/KÖLLING, HARTMUT: *Europäische Hieb- und Stichwaffen.* Berlin: Brandenburgisches Verlagshaus, 1981

NEUMANN, SARAH: *Der gerichtliche Zweikampf: Gottesurteil – Wettstreit – Ehrensache.* Ostfildern: Jan Thorbecke Verlag, 2010

NICKEL, HELMUT: *Ullstein Waffenbuch.* Frankfurt/M., Berlin, Wien: Ullstein, 1974

NORMAN, VESEY: *Waffen und Rüstungen.* Stuttgart: Parkland

NOTTARP, HERMANN: *Gottesurteile.* Bamberg: Bamberger Verlagshaus Meisenbach & Co., 1949

NOWAKOWSKI, ANDRZEJ: *Arms and Armour in the Medieval Teutonic Order's State in Prussia.* Łódź: Oficyna Naukowa MS, 1994

OAKESHOTT, EWART: *The Archaeology of Weapons: Arms and Armour from Prehistory to the Age of Chivalry.* New York: Frederick A. Praeger, 1960

OAKESHOTT, EWART: *The Sword in the Age of Chivalry.* London: Lutterworth Press, 1964

OAKESHOTT, EWART: *Records of the Medieval Sword.* Woodbridge: Boydell Press, 1991

OAKESHOTT, EWART: *A Knight and His Weapon.* Dufour Editions: Chester Springs, Pennsylvania, 1997

OAKESHOTT, EWART: *A Knight and His Armor.* Dufour Editions: Chester Springs, Pennsylvania, 1999

OAKESHOTT, EWART: *European Weapons and Armour.* Woodbridge: Boydell Press, 2000

OAKESHOTT, EWART: *Sword in Hand. A Brief Survey of the Medieval Sword.* Minneapolis: Arms & Armor, 2000

PAGGIARINO, CARLO: *The Churburg Armoury.* Milan: Hans Prunner Editore, 2006

PAGGIARINO, CARLO: *The Wallace Collection.* Milan: Hans Prunner Editore, 2008

PORZIO, LUCA/MELE, GREGORY: *Arte gladiatoria dimicandi.* Union City, California: Chivalry Bookshelf, 2002

REITZENSTEIN, ALEXANDER FREIHERR VON: *Der Waffenschmied.* Munich: Prestel, 1964

RUBBOLI, MARCO/CESARI, LUCA: *Flos Duellatorum.* Rimini: Il Cerchio Iniziative Editoriali, 2002

ŠACH, JAN: *Illustriertes Lexikon der Hieb- & Stichwaffen.* Erlangen: Karl Müller Verlag, 1999

SCHAER, ALFRED: *Die altdeutschen Fechter und Spielleute.* Strasbourg: Karl J. Trübner, 1901

SCHLUNK, ANDREAS/GIERSCH, ROBERT: *Die Ritter. Geschichte – Kultur – Alltagsleben.* Stuttgart: Konrad Theiss Verlag, 2003

SCHULZE, ANDRÉ: *Mittelalterliche Kampfesweisen. Das Lange Schwert.* Mainz: Philipp von Zabern, 2006

SCHULZE, ANDRÉ (ED.): *Mittelalterliche Kampfesweisen. Scheibendolch und Stechschild.* Mainz: Philipp von Zabern, 2007

SCHULZE, ANDRÉ (ED.): *Mittelalterliche Kampfesweisen. Der Kriegshammer, Schild und Kolben.* Mainz: Philipp von Zabern, 2007

STONE, GEORGE CAMERON: *A Glossary of the Construction, Decoration and Use of Arms and Armor.* Portland, Maine: Southwork Press, 1934

STUDER, CHARLES: *Das Solothurner Fechtbuch.* Solothurn: Zentralbibliothek Solothurn

TALHOFFER, HANS: *Talhoffers Fechtbuch.* Herne: VS-Books, 1998

THOMAS, BRUNO: *Deutsche Plattnerkunst.* Munich: F. Bruckmann, 1944

THOMAS, BRUNO: *Harnische.* Vienna: Kunstverlag Wolfrum, 1947

THOMAS, BRUNO/GAMBER, ORTWIN/SCHEDELMANN, HANS: *Die schönsten Waffen und Rüstungen aus europäischen und amerikanischen Sammlungen.* Heidelberg, Munich: Keysersche Verlagsbuchhandlung, 1963

TOBLER, CHRISTIAN HENRY: *In Service of the Duke: The 15th century fighting treatise of Paulus Kal.* Highland Village, Texas: Chivalry Bookshelf, 2006

TOBLER, CHRISTIAN HENRY: *In Saint George's Name. An Anthology of Medieval German Fighting Arts.* Wheaton, Illinois: Freelance Academy Press, 2010

TOBLER, CHRISTIAN HENRY: *Captain of the Guild. Master Peter Falkner's Art of Knightly Defense.* Wheaton, Illinois: Freelance Academy Press, 2011

WAGNER, EDUARD/DROBNÁ, ZOROSLAVA/DURDÍK, JAN: *Tracht, Wehr und Waffen.* Prague: Artia, 1960

WALCZAK, BARTŁOMIEJ/HAGEDORN, DIERK: *Gladiatoria.* Pelplin: Orbis Pictus, 2014

WELLE, RAINER: *»... und wisse das alle höbischeit kompt von deme ringen«.* Pfaffenweiler: Centaurus, 1993

WELLE, RAINER: *... vnd mit der rechten faust ein mordstuck – Baumanns Fecht- und Ringkampfhandschrift.* Munich: Herbert Utz Verlag, 2014

WIERSCHIN, MARTIN: *Meister Johann Liechtenauers Kunst des Fechtens.* Munich: C. H. Beck'sche Verlagsbuchhandlung, 1965

WOOSNAM-SAVAGE, ROBERT/HALL, ANTHONY: *Brassey's Book of Body Armor.* Dulles, Virginia: Brassey's, 2001

ŻABIŃSKI, GRZEGORZ/WALCZAK, BARTŁOMIEJ: *Codex Wallerstein: A Medieval Fighting Book from the Fifteenth Century.* Boulder, Colorado: Paladin Press, 2002

V.
Dependent Publications

BENARY, WALTER: "Ein unbekanntes handschriftliches Fragment einer Lope'schen Komödie". *Zeitschrift für Romanische Philologie,* Band 36, Heft 6, 1912

EHWALD, RUDOLF: *Chart. B 1974.* Gotha: Forschungsbibliothek

GOLL, MATTHIAS/MÜLLER, PETER/GRAF, DIETER: "Die älteste deutsche Harnischbrust. Ein Sensationsfund?" *Waffen- und Kostümkunde,* Heft 1, 2008

HILS, HANS-PETER: "Die Handschriften des oberdeutschen Fechtmeisters Hans Talhoffer". *Codices manuscripti,* Heft 3, 1983

HILS, HANS-PETER: "'Gladiatoria'. Über drei Fechthandschriften aus der ersten Hälfte des 15. Jahrhunderts". *Codices manuscripti,* Heft 1/2, 1987

Hils, Hans-Peter: “Reflexionen zum Stand der hauptberuflichen Fechter des Späten Mittelalters unter Berücksichtigung historischer Rechtsquellen”. *Würzburger medizinhistorische Forschungen,* Band 38, 1994

Jaquet, Daniel/Walczak, Bartłomiej: “Liegnitzer, Hundsfeld or Lew? The question of authorship of popular medieval fighting teachings”. *Acta periodica duellatorum,* vol. 2, 2014

Mann, James: “Notes on the Evolution of Plate Armour in Germany in the Fourteenth and Fifteenth Century”. *Society of Antiquaries of London,* 1935

Schwietering, Julius: “Zur Geschichte von Speer und Schwert im 12. Jahrhundert”. *Mitteilungen aus dem Museum für Hamburgische Geschichte,* Nr. 3, 1912

Stangier, Thomas: “Ich hab ein hertz als ein leb...” *Ritterwelten im Spätmittelalter.* Landshut: Schriften aus den Museen der Stadt Landshut, 2009

Wanke, Tilman: “Anderthalbhänder – Zweihänder – Langes Schwert”. *Waffen- und Kostümkunde,* Heft 2, 2009

VI.
Catalogues and Guides

Gamber, Ortwin/Beaufort, Christian: *Katalog der Leibrüstkammer. II. Teil: Der Zeitraum vom 1530 bis 1560.* Busto Arsizio: Bramante Editrice, 1990

Mann, James: *Wallace Collection Catalogues. European Arms and Armour.* London: Trustees of the Wallace Collection, 1962

Quaas, Gerhard (ed.): *Eisenkleider.* Berlin, DHM, 1992

Schneider, Hugo/Stüber, Karl: *Waffen im Schweizerischen Landesmuseum. Griffwaffen I.* Zurich: Orell Füssli, 1980

Thomas, Bruno/Gamber, Ortwin: *Katalog der Leibrüstkammer. I. Teil: Der Zeitraum vom 500 bis 1530.* Vienna: Anton Schroll & Co., 1976

Die Innsbrucker Plattnerkunst. Katalog. Tiroler Landesmuseum Ferdinandeum, 1954

Das Wiener Bürgerliche Zeughaus. Rüstungen und Waffen aus 5 Jahrhunderten. Eigenverlag der Museen der Stadt Wien, 1977

Harnische. Historisches Museum. Staatliche Kunstsammlungen Dresden

VII.
Online Sources: Transcriptions

BACHMANN, DIETER: *Best. 7020.* wiktenauer.com

BACHMANN, DIETER: *Talhoffer 1459. Thott 290 2° – Meister Hans Talhoffers alte Armatur und Ringkunst.* wiktenauer.com

GOSEWINKEL, JAN: *Paulus Hector Mair – Mscr.Dresd.C.94.* hammaborg.de, 2011

HAGEDORN, DIERK: *Peter von Danzig – Codex 44 A 8.* hammaborg.de, 2006

HAGEDORN, DIERK: *Paulus Kal – Cgm 1507.* hammaborg.de, 2007

HAGEDORN, DIERK: *Cod. Hs. 3227a.* hammaborg.de, 2008

HAGEDORN, DIERK: *Sigmund Ringeck – Mscr. Dresd. C 487.* hammaborg.de, 2008

HAGEDORN, DIERK: *Jude Lew – Cod.I.6.4°.3.* hammaborg.de, 2008

HAGEDORN, DIERK: *Hans von Speyer – M.I.29.* hammaborg.de, 2008

HAGEDORN, DIERK: *"Gladiatoria" – MS U860.F46.1450.* hammaborg.de, 2009

HAGEDORN, DIERK: *Jörg Wilhalm – Cod.I.6.4°.5.* hammaborg.de, 2009

HAGEDORN, DIERK: *Jörg Wilhalm – I.6.2°.3.* hammaborg.de, 2009

HAGEDORN, DIERK: *Jörg Wilhalm, Lienhart Sollinger – I.6.2°.2.* hammaborg.de, 2009

HAGEDORN, DIERK: *E.1939.65.341.* hammaborg.de, 2009

HAGEDORN, DIERK: *Peter Falkner – KK 5012.* hammaborg.de, 2009

HAGEDORN, DIERK: *Hans Talhoffer – 78 A 15.* hammaborg.de, 2009

HAGEDORN, DIERK: *Hans Talhoffer – Ms. Chart. A 558.* hammaborg.de, 2009

HAGEDORN, DIERK: *Hans Talhoffer – Hs. XIX, 17-3.* hammaborg.de, 2010

HAGEDORN, DIERK: *"Gladiatoria" – 78.2 Aug. 2°.* hammaborg.de, 2010

HAGEDORN, DIERK: *Libr. pict. A. 83.* hammaborg.de, 2011

KLEINAU, JENS PETER: *Libr. pict. A. 83.* talhoffer.wordpress.com, 2011

KOHUTOVIČ, ANTON: *Best. 7020.* gesellschaft-lichtenawers.eu

KOHUTOVIČ, ANTON: *Paulus Hector Mair - Codex Vindobonensis 10825/26.* gesell schaft-lichtenawers.eu, 2002

KOHUTOVIČ, ANTON: *Codex Wallerstein (Cod.I.6.4°.2).* gesellschaft-lichtenawers. eu, 2010

KOHUTOVIČ, ANTON: *Sigmund Emring (Ringeck). 1508. E.1939.65.341. Transcription.* gesellschaft-lichtenawers.eu, 2010

VIII.
Additional Online Sources

Bildarchiv Foto Marburg: *Bildindex der Kunst und Architektur.* bildindex.de
Effigies & Brasses: effigiesandbrasses.com
Fechtgeschichte: fechtgeschichte.blogspot.de
Historische Waffen Jürgen H. Fricker: fricker-historische-waffen.de
Hans Talhoffer: talhoffer.wordpress.com
Hroarr: *Resources for the Historical European Martial Arts.* hroarr.com
Trier Center for Digital Humanities: *Wörterbuchnetz.* woerterbuchnetz.de
Wiktenauer: *The free library of Historical European Martial Arts books and manuscripts.* wiktenauer.com

All online sources last visited on January 17, 2018